# Executive Compensation in ESOP Companies

# Executive Compensation in ESOP Companies

The National Center for Employee Ownership
Oakland, California

**Executive Compensation in ESOP Companies**
Book design by Scott S. Rodrick

The National Center for Employee Ownership
1736 Franklin Street, 8th Floor
Oakland, CA 94612
(510) 208-1300
(510) 272-9510 (fax)
E-mail: *nceo@nceo.org*
Web: *http://www.nceo.org/*

First published in November 2005

ISBN: 1-932924-15-9

# Contents

# Preface

**E**xecutive compensation in ESOP companies has become a much
more complex issue in recent years. As many companies switch
to subchapter S status, they must be careful to avoid the draconian tax penalties under the anti-abuse sections of the law that can be
triggered by poorly drawn plans. The Sarbanes-Oxley Act, while applying only to public companies, is raising the corporate governance bar
for many closely held companies as well. And the new deferred compensation rules require careful planning to avoid significant tax penalties for companies and executives alike.

The good news is that all these problems can be successfully avoided
with proper planning and an understanding of how the rules work.
One of the goals of this book is to help companies understand just
what they need to do to comply with the rules and plan ahead.

But there is much more to executive compensation than comply-
ing with the rules or maximizing tax benefits. Under ERISA, the ESOP
trustee has an obligation to be an involved shareholder and ensure that
company assets are not wasted on excessive or unjustified executive
compensation. At the same time, the trustee wants to ensure that executive compensation plans are adequate to attract and retain qualified, motivated key employees. Boards of directors share the same
concerns, of course, and have a fiduciary responsibility to shareholders
to strike the right balance. So in addition to exploring the rules for

executive compensation, the chapters in this book help ESOP companies find the best strategies for executive compensation.

Finally, this book includes a report on the first-ever survey of executive compensation in ESOP companies. The results strongly suggest that ESOP companies have a much more restrained approach to executive compensation than many of their non-ESOP peers. Executives in ESOP companies make less than their peers in similar non-ESOP companies, both in current and deferred compensation. As many of the survey respondents noted, however, executives also have a substantial stake in the ESOP, something not counted in this survey (qualified retirement plan contributions normally are not considered in such calculations).

There is no simple solution to executive compensation in ESOP companies, of course. While surveys are useful, few people simply want to do what everyone else does just because it is the norm. While one company might find that an emphasis on short-term incentive pay is the best approach, another might want to emphasize equity compensation or long-term deferred pay. We hope this book will help companies find just which path works.

# CHAPTER 1

# Sharing Equity with Key Employees in ESOP Companies

Corey Rosen

**M**any ESOP companies, both publicly traded and privately held, want to provide employees with a stake in the company as an incentive or reward for their work. While giving employees cash bonuses, profit sharing, extra vacation, a company car, or other perquisites can be highly valued, sharing equity is unique in its ability to link the employee's interests to the long-term growth of company value. Because equity plans can so easily be designed to require employees to earn their shares through future years of service or meeting certain performance targets, they also can be ideal mechanisms for getting employees to focus on long-term goals—and to stay around long enough to make sure those goals are met.

ESOP companies already share equity with key employees, of course, through the plan itself. The NCEO survey of executive compensation in ESOP companies found that most companies see this as sufficient. Some pay additional cash incentives, such as bonuses or profit sharing. Others provide insurance plans or other deferred compensation. These approaches are generally straightforward and do not require any elaborate legal exploration or detail. But they may also not provide a sufficient incentive to attract, retain, and motivate people who, in another company, might be able to command more equity than the ESOP provides. This chapter is not an argument that companies should do this; that is a matter of corporate philosophy and needs. It does look at the basic issues involved for companies that do choose this approach. This chapter does not discuss the fiduciary issues involved in providing equity to key employees (see the chapter on fiduciary issues for details), and only briefly describes the new deferred compensation rules (see the chapter by Alan Nadel and Virginia Bartlett on compensating ESOP executives for details on this) and accounting rules.

The individual equity plans described here, including stock options, restricted stock and restricted stock units, phantom stock, and stock appreciation rights, can be given to any employee under any set of criteria. In return for this flexibility, these plans do not carry significant tax benefits, with the exception of incentive stock options (ISOs). The employee's gains from ISOs can be taxed as capital gains, but the company then gives up any tax deduction.

This chapter is not a substitute for detailed investigation of the particular plans chosen. All of these plans involve often complex tax, accounting, planning, administration, financing, and feasibility issues. Instead, this chapter provides a very basic overview to help decision-makers understand the array of choices available.

## Basic Forms of Individual Equity Plans

There are four basic kinds of individual equity compensation plans: stock options, restricted stock and restricted stock units, stock appreciation rights, and phantom stock. Some of these plans have variations as well. Each plan provides employees with some special consideration in price or terms. We do not cover here simply offering employees the right to buy stock as any other investor would.

*Stock options* give employees the right to buy a number of shares at a price fixed at grant for a defined number of years into the future. *Restricted stock* (and its close relative *restricted stock units*) give employees the right to acquire or receive shares, by gift or purchase, once certain restrictions, such as working a certain number of years or meeting a performance target, are met. *Phantom stock* pays a future cash bonus equal to the value of a certain number of shares. *Stock appreciation rights* (SARs) provide the right to the increase in the value of a designated number of shares, usually paid in cash, but occasionally settled in shares (this is called a "stock-settled SAR").

## Stock Options

A few key concepts help define how stock options work:

- *Exercise:* The purchase of stock with an option.

- *Exercise price:* The price at which the stock can be purchased. This is also called the *strike price* or *grant price*. In most plans, the exercise price is the current fair market value of the stock at the time the grant is made.

- *Spread:* The difference between the exercise price and the market value of the stock at the time of exercise.

- *Option term:* The length of time the employee can hold the option before it expires.

- *Vesting:* The process by which the right to exercise options is earned, usually by years of service.

A company grants an employee options to buy a stated number of shares at a defined grant price. The options vest over a period of time or once certain individual, group, or corporate goals are met. Once vested, the employee can exercise the option at the grant price at any time over the option term up to the expiration date. For instance, an employee might be granted the right to buy 1,000 shares at $10 per share. The options vest 25% per year over four years and have a term of 10 years. If the stock goes up, the employee will pay $10 per share to buy the stock. The difference between the $10 grant price and the exercise price is the spread. If the stock goes to $25 after seven years, and the employee exercises all options, the spread would be $15 per share.

### Kinds of Options

Option plans are either incentive stock options (ISOs) or nonqualified options (NSOs). When an employee exercises a nonqualified stock option, the spread on exercise is taxable to the employee as ordinary income, even if the shares are not yet sold. A corresponding amount is deductible by the company. There is no legally required holding period for the shares after exercise, although the company may impose one. Any subsequent gain or loss on the shares after exercise is taxed as a capital gain or loss.

An incentive stock option (ISO) enables an employee to (1) defer taxation on the option from the date of exercise until the date of sale of the underlying shares, and (2) pay tax at capital gains rates, rather than ordinary income tax rates, on the spread at exercise. Certain conditions must be met to qualify for ISO treatment:

1.  The employee must hold the stock for at least one year after the exercise date or two years after the grant date, whichever is later.

2.  Only $100,000 of stock options can first become exercisable in any year. This is measured by the grant price of the options, not the exercise price. It means that only $100,000 in grant price value can vest (first become exercisable) in any one year. If there is overlapping vesting, such as would occur if options are granted annually and vest gradually, companies must track outstanding options to see whether the amount that becomes vested under different grants will exceed $100,000 in grant value in any one year.

3.  The exercise price must not be less than the market price of the company's stock on the date of the grant.

4.  Only employees can qualify for ISOs.

5.  The option must be granted pursuant to a written plan that has been approved by shareholders and that specifies how many shares can be issued under the plan and identifies the class of employees eligible to receive the options. Options must be granted within 10 years of the date of the adoption of the plan.

6.  The option must be exercised within 10 years of the date of the grant.

7.  The employee cannot own, at the time of the grant, more than 10% of the voting power of all outstanding stock of the company, unless the exercise price is at least 110% of the market value of the stock on the date of the grant and the option is not exercisable more than five years from the date of the grant.

8.  ISOs can only be issued to employees.

If all the rules for incentive options are met at the time of exercise, then the transaction is called a "qualifying disposition," and the employee pays capital gains tax on the total increase in value at sale over the grant price. However, the spread on the option at exercise is a "preference item" for purposes of the alternative minimum tax (AMT). So even though the shares may not have been sold, the exercise requires the employee to add back the gain on exercise, along with other AMT preference items, to see whether an alternative minimum tax payment is due.

The company does not take a tax deduction when there is a qualifying disposition. If, however, there is a disqualifying disposition, most often because the employee exercises and sells before meeting the required holding periods, the spread on exercise is taxable to the employee at ordinary income tax rates, and any capital appreciation on the ISO shares in excess of the market price on exercise is taxed at capital gains rates. In this instance, the company may then deduct the spread on exercise.

The second kind of option is a nonqualified option (NSO). NSOs can be issued to anyone—employees, directors, consultants, suppliers, customers, etc. There are no special tax benefits for NSOs, however. Like an ISO, there is no tax on the grant of the option, but when it is exercised, the spread between the grant and exercise price is taxable as ordinary income. The company receives a corresponding tax deduction. Note: if the exercise price of the NSO is less than fair market value, it is subject to the deferred compensation rules under Section 409A of the Internal Revenue Code and may be taxed at vesting and subject to penalties.

### Exercising an Option

There are four ways to exercise a stock option: cash, the exchange of existing shares (often called a stock swap), same-day sales, and their close relative, sell-to-cover sales (these latter two are often called cashless exercises, although that term actually includes other exercise methods described here as well). Any one company, however, may provide for just one or two of these alternatives. Private companies do not offer same-day or sell-to-cover sales, and, not infrequently, restrict the exercise or sale of the shares acquired through exercise until the company is sold or goes public.

The most common form of exercise for an option in a closely held company is simply for the employee to pay cash for the shares. The employee might then have additional taxes due, depending on the kind of option. If the options are nonqualified, the employer might then have to withhold taxes on the spread from the employee's future paychecks, unless the employer can arrange to use some of the option shares to pay for this obligation, as would normally be the case in the kind of cashless transactions described below.

In a same-day sale, the employee works with a broker, usually one provided by the company. The company provides the broker with enough shares to cover the option exercise, the broker turns around and sells them, and the proceeds, minus the exercise price and any taxes due, go to the employee. Although called a "same-day" sale, the process can take up to three days. In a sell-to-cover exercise, the same approach is used, but the broker sells only enough shares to cover the exercise price and any taxes due, giving the employee the remaining value in shares.

In a stock swap, the employee simply exchanges existing shares for the option shares. For instance, if the employee has the right to buy 1,000 shares at $10 per share, and the shares are now worth $25, the employee would exchange 400 shares the employee currently owns for the 1,000 shares. That's because the 400 shares the employee owns are worth $10,000. The employee would then get 600 shares from the option. If there are taxes due as well, then the employee might choose to turn in enough shares to cover the taxes as well, although this would not be a common strategy. Stock swaps are more commonly used with incentive stock options where taxes do not have to be paid until the newly acquired shares are sold.

### Accounting

Under rules for equity compensation plans to be effective in 2005 (FASB Statement 123R), companies must calculate the present value of all option awards as of the date of grant and show this as a charge to compensation. The value should be adjusted based on vesting experience (so unvested shares do not count as a charge to compensation).

Publicly traded companies must adopt the standard by their first interim or annual fiscal period beginning after June 15, 2005 (December 15, 2005, for small business issuers). The new standard applies to any options and other equity awards granted after adoption and any options or awards granted before adoption that are not yet vested. Privately held companies must adopt the standard by their first annual fiscal period beginning after December 15, 2005. For privately held companies that currently use a minimum value model to account for stock options under SFAS No. 123, the new standard applies only to options and awards granted after adoption; it does not apply to any options or awards granted prior to adoption. In addition, these companies are not permitted to voluntarily restate prior fiscal periods.

## Deferred Compensation Rules

Employees could always defer the receipt of a vested (and thus taxable) equity award under deferred compensation plans by making an election. Rules for how to do this have been ambiguous. Under the 2004 tax law, employees will be able to elect to defer only if several conditions are met:

1.  The employee dies, becomes disabled, there is a change in control, there is an unforeseen emergency (as rigorously defined in the law), or there is a fixed date or schedule specified by the plan.

2.  Elections for deferral must be made not later than the close of the preceding taxable year in which the award would vest or, if made in the first year of the award, within 30 days after the employee first becomes eligible for an award. If the employee is a key employee (as defined by statute) of a public company, receipt of the benefit must be not earlier than six months after separation.

3.  If the award is performance-based, the election must come not later than six months before the end of the performance period.

4.  There can be no acceleration of benefits once a deferral election has been made.

5.  Any subsequent elections for an award must be at least 12 months after the prior election and must defer receipt for at least five years in the future.

The law does not apply to qualified benefit plans, such as ESOPs or 401(k) plans, as well as sick leave, death benefits, and similar arrangements. Existing rules for incentive stock options would not be changed, and nonqualified options would not be covered provided that they are not issued at less than fair market value. The effective date is December 31, 2004, but deferrals made after October 2, 2004, under a plan that has been materially modified after that date would be covered. ESPPs are not subject to the new deferred compensation plan rules.

*Valuation*

Under the new deferred compensation plan rules, to determine whether a nonqualified option is issued at fair market value in a closely held company, a company must establish a mechanism to know what fair market value is. Similarly, under regulations issued in 2004 for incentive stock options, to meet the "$100,000 rule," closely held companies also have to establish a fair market value. Unfortunately, there is no specific guidance on just what the IRS would allow as an acceptable valuation technique. There is a safe harbor method of using two independent appraisals contemporaneous with the issuance of each award, but few closely held companies will want to do that. Most advisors believe that a single independent appraisal would probably suffice, or even a rigorous process established by the board, but there is no certainty about this. In an ESOP company, therefore, it would make sense to time the grant of options closely with the effective date of the ESOP appraisal and use the same price. The rigorous requirements of ERISA for ESOP valuations would seem to provide a convincing argument that this amount is justifiable for option purposes.

## Restricted Stock

Restricted stock plans provide employees with the right to purchase shares at fair market value or a discount, or it simply grants shares to employees outright. However, the shares employees acquire are not really theirs yet—they cannot take possession of the shares until specified restrictions lapse. Most commonly, the restriction is that the employee work for the company for a certain number of years, often three to five. The time-based restrictions may pass all at once or gradually. Any restrictions could be imposed, however. The company could, for instance, restrict the shares until certain corporate, departmental, or individual performance goals are achieved. With restricted stock units (RSUs), employees do not actually buy or receive shares *until* the restrictions lapse. In effect, RSUs are like phantom stock settled in shares instead of cash.

While the shares are subject to restrictions, companies can choose whether to pay dividends, provide voting rights, or give the employee other benefits of being a shareholder. When employees are awarded the restricted stock, they have the right to make what is called a "Section 83(b)" election, much as they can make this election for a stock option. If they make the election, they are taxed at ordinary income tax rates on the "bargain element" of the award at the time of grant. If the shares are simply granted to the employee, then the bargain element is their full value. If some consideration is paid, then the tax is based on the difference between what is paid and the fair market value at the time of the grant. If full price is paid, there is no tax. Any future increase in the value of the shares until they are sold is then taxed as capital gains, not ordinary income. If employees do not make the election, then there is no tax until the restrictions lapse, at which time ordinary income tax is due on the difference between the grant and exercise price. Subsequent changes in value are capital gains (or losses). RSUs do not allow employees to make the Section 83(b) election.

The employer gets a tax deduction only for amounts employees pay income tax on, regardless of whether a Section 83(b) election is made or not. A Section 83(b) election carries some risk. If the employee makes the election and pays tax, but the restrictions never lapse, the employee does not get the taxes paid refunded, nor does the employee get the shares.

Restricted stock accounting parallels option accounting in most respects. If the only restriction is vesting, companies account for restricted stock by first determining the total compensation cost at the time the award is made. So if the employee is simply given 1,000 restricted shares worth $10 per share, then a $10,000 cost is incurred. If the employee buys the shares at fair value, no charge is recorded; if there is a discount, that counts as a cost. The cost is then amortized over the period of vesting until the restrictions lapse. Because the accounting is based on the initial cost, companies with a low share price will find that a vesting requirement for the award means their accounting charge will be very low even if the stock price goes up.

If the award is more contingent, such as performance vesting, the value must be adjusted each year for the current stock price, then amortized over the estimated life of the award (the time estimated to meet the performance goal). Each year, the expected cost is amortized over the estimated remaining expected life. So if the stock is awarded at $10 and goes to $15 in the first year of an expected five-year term, then $15 × 1,000 × .20 is recorded ($3,000). If the price goes to $18 the next year, the calculation is $18 × 1,000 × .40 ($7,200). The prior $3,000 is subtracted from this amount, yielding a charge of $4,200 for that year.

Restricted stock is not subject to the new deferred compensation plan rules, but restricted stock units are.

## Phantom Stock and Stock Appreciation Rights

Stock appreciation rights (SARs) and phantom stock are very similar plans. Both essentially are cash bonus plans, although some plans pay out the benefits in the form of shares. SARs typically provide the employee with a cash payment based on the increase in the value of a stated number of shares over a specific period of time. Phantom stock provides a cash or stock bonus based on the value of a stated number of shares, to be paid out at the end of a specified period of time. SARs may not have a specific settlement date; like options, the employees may have flexibility in when to choose to exercise the SAR. Phantom stock may pay dividends; SARs would not. When the payout is made, it is taxed as ordinary income to the employee and is deductible to the employer. Some phantom plans condition the receipt of the award on meeting certain objectives, such as sales, profits, or other targets. These plans often refer to their phantom stock as "performance units." Phantom stock and SARs can be given to anyone, but if they are given out broadly to employees, there is a possibility that they will be considered retirement plans and will be subject to federal retirement plan rules. Careful plan structuring can avoid this problem.

Because SARs and phantom plans are essentially cash bonuses or are delivered in the form of stock that holders will want to cash in, companies need to figure out how to pay for them. Does the company just make a promise to pay, or does it really put aside the funds? If the award is paid in stock, is there a market for the stock? If it is only a promise, will employees believe the benefit is as phantom as the stock? If it is in real funds set aside for this purpose, the company will be putting after-tax dollars aside and not in the business. Many small, growth-oriented companies cannot afford to do this. The fund can also be subject to excess accumulated earnings tax. On the other hand, if employees are given shares, the shares can be paid for by capital markets if the company goes public or by acquirers if the company is sold.

If phantom stock or SARs are irrevocably promised to employees, it is possible the benefit will become taxable before employees actually receive the funds. A "rabbi trust," a segregated account to fund deferred payments to employees, may help solve the accumulated earnings problem, but if the company is unable to pay creditors with existing funds, the money in these trusts goes to them. Telling employees their right to the benefit is not irrevocable or is dependent on some condition (working another five years, for instance) may prevent the money from being currently taxable, but it may also weaken employee belief that the benefit is real.

Phantom stock and SAR accounting is straightforward. When the awards are settled in cash, these plans are treated in the same way as deferred cash compensation. As the amount of the liability changes each year, an entry is made for the amount accrued. A decline in value would create a negative entry. These entries are not contingent on vesting. In closely held companies, share value is often stated as book value. However, this can dramatically underrate the true value of a company, especially one based primarily on intellectual capital. Having an outside appraisal performed, therefore, can make the plans much more accurate rewards for employee contributions.

If phantom stock or SAR awards are settled in stock, the accounting is more similar to stock option accounting. A present value estimate of the award cost must be made at grant, and it can be adjusted later to correct for forfeitures.

Phantom stock and SARs settled in cash, as well as grants of SARs settled in stock in closely held companies, are also now subject to deferred compensation rules under Section 409A of the Internal Revenue Code. These rules require employees to make an election to defer receipt of an award after vesting to not later than the last day of the year before the year the award vests. If an award vests in June 2010, for instance, the election would have to be made by December 31, 2008. If vesting is based on performance, the election can be made up to six months before.

SARs are not subject to the new deferred compensation plans if they are settled in stock in public companies. Cash-settled SARs and phantom stock are subject to the new rules. SARs in public companies only qualify, however, if:

- The exercise price is never less than the fair market value at grant.
- There is no additional deferral provision.
- The SAR is not part of a tandem arrangement with a stock option under which the SAR is paid in cash; in that case, the option will be considered deferred compensation.

SARs granted before Oct. 3, 2004, are excluded for closely held companies as well if they meet the last three rules.

## Designing an Equity Incentive Plan

Designing an individual equity plan requires a variety of issues to be considered. This section is not intended to provide specific guidelines on how to structure a plan but rather to raise the issues companies need to consider. In making these decisions, company leaders should consult with peers and advisors as well as evaluate available survey data on industry practices.

### How Much to Share

The first decision is how much ownership to share. The most typical way a decision is made about how much ownership to share in a closely held ESOP company is to set aside an amount of stock that is within the maximum dilution level acceptable to the board and the ESOP trustee. This approach can create problems, however.

Typically, once this number is set, a large portion of those shares is either provided immediately to existing employees, or they are allocated to employees over a certain number of years. The problem with this strategy is that if the company grows faster than anticipated, there are no or relatively few shares left to give to new employees. That can be a severe problem in attracting and retaining good people. It can also create two classes of employees, some with large equity grants and some without them. Moreover, this model often does not create an explicit link between employee effort and the rewards of ownership.

A second approach focuses on what percentage of compensation it is necessary to provide in the form of equity in order to attract, retain, and motivate people. These decisions need to be based on a sense of what people can get elsewhere, as well as discussions with employees to get a sense of how much they expect.

A third approach is to base the award on what seem like a reasonable percentage of the employee's compensation. This approach provides easier benchmarking with other companies.

Finally, a company could grant or vest awards based on performance. If the company, group, or individual meets certain targets, than x number of awards are provided and/or vested. Care must be taken in this model, however, to be sure that compensation does not exceed what is deemed "reasonable."

## What Kind of Equity?

Very small companies with no plans to be acquired or go public often want to use SARs or phantom plans because they are simple, do not require actual stock to be issued, and can be used to track equity changes in non-stock companies. They lack some of the connotation of ownership, however, and offer no favorable tax treatment. Stock options and restricted stock, by contrast, require that the company provide some form of liquidity for the shares, often through a public offering or sale, although companies can also simply arrange to repurchase the shares.

Restricted stock and restricted stock units deliver actual shares to employees, even if the stock price declines. There are pros and cons to this approach. On the one hand, employees do not end up with nothing just because share prices decline in the market generally. On the other hand, some have argued that restricted stock just provides "equity for breathing," and that it is thus less of an incentive than options or SARs. Restricted stock can cause more economic dilution than options or SARs (because options are only exercised if the price of the stock goes up), but it causes less dilution in terms of the number of shares outstanding. That is because the risk protection of restricted stock means that each share granted is worth more than each option or SAR. A ratio of one restricted stock share to three or four stock options is not uncommon, for instance.

Option plans can be just NSOs, just ISOs, or some of both. Plans aimed at key employees in closely held companies are often ISOs because these employees can greatly benefit from capital gains treatment, and they may demand such options to come to work for or stay with a company. ISOs also carry no tax consequence, other than AMT (albeit that can be a significant one), until they are sold, whereas NSOs are taxed at exercise. Lacking a ready market for shares, this can be a significant consideration for a closely held company. Of course, an ESOP can provide a market, making NSOs in ESOP companies more appealing than they would be absent an ESOP. Note, however, that sales of option or other award-based stock (other than stock purchased at fair market value) does not qualify for Section 1042 tax deferral treatment when sold to an ESOP.

## Merit and Other Formulas for Making Awards

Equity can be granted either according to some kind of merit judgment or on the basis of a universal rule, such as allocating annually or on the date of hire, promotion, or the achievement of an individual, group, or corporate objective. These methods are not mutually exclusive; many companies use a combination of these techniques.

A typical merit-based plan would provide work unit managers (or a single manager in a smaller company) with a number of awards that can be granted to employees in the group based on a performance appraisal. An alternative to individual merit judgments is to provide that a pool of equity awards will be given to a work team on the achievement of their own goals. Many companies, of course, will simply name specific individuals, usually top managers, who will get equity, but the company will define how much they get based on some merit assessment.

At the other end of the spectrum is an automatic formula based on compensation, seniority, promotion, or some other work-related, measurable construct. Providing awards on hiring, with additional grants on promotion or periodic refresher grants, is another common allocation rule. Linking additional grants to promotion gives employees an incentive to improve their skills and rewards those people the organization believes are making greater contributions. On the other hand, it can lose the attention of employees who may be very good performers but who are not in jobs that can easily lead to a promotion.

Refresher grants give employees additional awards when they exercise some of the options or other equity benefits they were previously granted. For instance, if an employee has 1,000 options and exercises 200, then the employee would be given new options on another 200 shares at exercise. The theory here is to maintain a constant level of equity interest in the company. Similarly, refresher awards might be granted when the company issues additional shares so that an employee maintains the same percentage of potential ownership as was held before the dilution (this feature would be more common for executive plans). While these automatic additional grants help to keep the employee's equity interest high, shareholders might object to the ongoing dilution.

### How Often Should Awards Be Granted?

Equity inherently involves risk, but the design of plans can accentuate that risk. Companies that provide one-time grants or grants on the attainment of an event, such as hiring, promotion, or meeting some corporate target, place most or all of an employee's ownership interest in the company based on the price of stock at a single point in time.

This practice accelerates the risk of equity both for the employee and the company. With options and SARs particularly, equity granted at a high price may never be "in the money"; awards given at a low price may cost the company more than it ever intended when they are redeemed. Employees who happen to get their chunk of equity at a good time end up doing very well, while those who have gotten their grants when the price was not so favorable, don't do well at all. Creating an ownership culture of "we're all in this together" can be very difficult in these circumstances.

For many companies, the best way to deal with these potential problems is to provide grants in smaller amounts but more frequently. This works best for companies using equity as a compensation strategy. Start-ups whose stock value is close to zero anyway or who use large initial grants to attract people away from other opportunities may find this less appropriate. It also won't work for companies that want simply to make grants at the occasional discretion of the company, often on the attainment of some corporate milestone. These companies see equity more as a symbolic reward than as ongoing ownership strategy.

Smaller but more frequent grants are easiest to do in public companies where the share price is readily ascertainable and where share prices change continually. In a closely held company, there would be no point in granting equity more frequently than the stock is valued. Giving an employee a grant three times a year when the price per share is determined annually, for instance, would give the employee three sets of awards all at the same price.

The periodic allocation "dollar-cost averages" the awards, smoothing bumps in volatile markets. This approach also gives employees more of a long-term, ongoing stake in the company. With the vesting schedules attached to the repeated grants of awards, employees are provided an even longer-term interest in the company's performance. Finally, there will be fewer big winners and losers among employees with otherwise similar jobs.

Frequent grants are not all good news, of course. The more often awards are granted, the more complex their administration becomes. Even with the best software, there will be much more data entry, many more forms to file and disseminate, and many more errors that can be made.

### When Will Employees Be Able to Use the Awards?

There are two principal issues in deciding when employees will be able to translate their equity into cash: vesting and exercise periods. Vesting generally provides that an employee accrues an increasing right to the awards granted based on the number of years worked. However, companies also sometimes use performance vesting, in which vesting is a function of company, group, or individual performance. As various targets are met, the equity awards becomes increasingly vested. The exercise period allows the employee to exercise or redeem an award for a defined number of years into the future once the award is vested.

The patterns on seniority-based vesting are fairly consistent across companies, with three to five-year graduated vesting the most common schedule. Sales or profit targets are the most common performance triggers. A more difficult decision is whether to provide for immediate vesting upon an event, such as going public or the sale of the company, even if the awards would not otherwise be vested. This clearly provides a good benefit for employees, but it may make it more difficult to sell a company or take one public, especially if buyers perceive that employees will now have fully vested options that, if they can also then be exercised, may be valuable enough so that some people will just walk away.

By far the most common exercise period for stock options is 10 years; there are no data on other plans. Some exercise periods are shorter, but they are rarely longer. There is nothing magical about 10 years for nonqualified options, but for incentive options, the exercise period cannot exceed 10 years. The more volatile a company's stock, the more important a longer exercise period is so that employees can weather the downturns. An alternative design used by a few companies allows employees to exercise their awards only when a defined event occurs, such as the achievement of a certain stock price or earnings goal. This accomplishes two things. First, it provides an incentive to meet the goal, and second, it reassures investors that dilution will only occur if the company meets certain targets. Once these targets are met, employees would normally be given a certain amount of time after the event to exercise the award, anywhere from a few months to several years. Alternatively, a company could provide that awards can be exercised only upon the occurrence of a stated event, such as a sale or going public.

Finally, the plan design should be specific in its compliance with applicable securities laws and stock exchange rules that can restrict certain employees from exercising equity awards or the sale of stock acquired from them by for a specified period after an IPO.

### Premium Pricing and Other Performance Bells and Whistles

Some companies are now looking at adding more performance triggers to their individual equity plans. As mentioned, vesting can be performance-triggered, as can the actual grant of an award (or the size of that grant). In addition, companies can use premium-priced awards, such as issuing an option at a grant price 10% above the current market price. In the executive compensation field, there are entire books written about formulas to base equity awards on performance. Another idea growing in popularity is indexed awards, where the award either only vests or is granted if the company's stock outperforms its peers. The details of these approaches are beyond the scope of this chapter, however. Suffice it to say that a common problem is picking a performance measure (EBITDA, economic value added, stock price growth, etc.) that does not really capture either what the executive can actually make happen or what is best for the company overall, or both.

## Securities Law Issues

If employees are given a right to purchase shares, the offer is subject to securities laws. ESOPs and 401(k) plans are not subject to most securities law requirements unless employees have a right to buy shares. The trust serves as the shareholder of record in these plans, and its ownership counts as one shareholder no matter how many people participate in the plan.

The two key elements of securities laws are registration and disclosure. Registration means the filing of documents with the state and/or federal securities agencies concerning the employer whose stock is being sold. There are registration procedures for small offerings of stock (under $1 million or $5 million, depending on the procedure) that can be done for relatively small legal fees (as little as $10,000 in some cases), but larger offerings require a lot of complex paperwork and fees often exceed $100,000. Registration requires the filing of audited financial statements and continuing reporting obligations to the federal Securities and Exchange Commission (SEC) and appropriate state agencies.

Disclosure refers to providing information to buyers about what they are getting, similar to, but frequently less detailed than, what would be in a prospectus. At times, there are specific state and federal rules about what needs to go in these documents, including objective discussions of risks, the financial condition of the firm, officers' and directors' salaries, and other information. In the absence of requirements for the registration of the securities, disclosure is intended to satisfy the anti-fraud requirements of federal and state laws.

Generally, offers to sell securities (stocks, bonds, etc.) require registration of those securities unless there is a specific exemption. In addition, corporations with 500 or more shareholders are considered public companies under federal law and must comply with the reporting requirements of the Exchange Act of 1934 even if they do not have to register under the Securities Act of 1933. For the purpose of counting shareholders, holders of unexercised options or restricted stock are included.

There are a number of exemptions from these rules. These are exemptions from registration; anytime stock is offered, it should include appropriate financial disclosure to satisfy anti-fraud rules.

The most important exemption is Rule 701. Under federal law, offers to a company's employees, directors, general partners, trustees, officers, or certain consultants (those providing services to a company similar to what an employer might hire someone to do, but not consultants who help raise capital) can be made under a written compensation agreement. If total sales during a 12-month period do not exceed the greater of $1 million, 15% of the issuer's total assets, or 15% of all the outstanding securities of that class, then the offerings are exempt from registration requirements. The offerings must be discrete (not included in any other offer) and are still subject to disclosure requirements. For total sales under $5 million during a 12-month period to the specified class of people above, companies must comply with anti-fraud disclosure rules; for sales over this amount, companies must disclose additional information, including risk factors, copies of the plans under which the offerings are made, and certain financial statements. These disclosures must be made to all shareholders.

For purposes of this rule, options are considered part of the aggregate sales price, with the option price defined as of the date of grant. In calculating outstanding securities for the 15% rule, all currently exercisable or convertible options, warrants, restricted stock, stock rights, and other securities are counted.

Other exemptions are available for sale to a limited number of accredited or sophisticated investors with appropriate information (these terms are legally defined and generally include officers, directors, and/or higher-income individuals); small offerings to 35 or fewer nonaccredited investors; offerings under $500,000; and offerings only to in-state residents if the offeror does 80% or more of its business and has 80% or more of its assets in-state.

These exemptions from registration are available under federal law. Some states track federal exemptions; some do not. Most states model their "blue sky laws" (the general name for state securities laws) on the Uniform Securities Act or the Revised Uniform Securities Act, which are partly based on federal law. Perhaps most importantly for offerings to employees, however, states that have a specific exemption parallel to the federal Rule 701 exemption (for offerings to employees) are the exception rather than the rule. State registration for such offerings may be needed, therefore, unless other exemptions are met.

Public companies cannot use Rule 701 for an exemption from securities law filings. Instead, most rely on Form S-8, a simplified registration form that can be used to comply with securities laws in conjunction with an offering of options. Public companies do not have to offer a formal prospectus to potential buyers, as closely held companies would. They are, however, required to provide information to employee stock purchasers about the company and its option plan. The S-8 form allows that to be done by reference to already available public documents.

Public companies must also make sure their plan design complies with trading restrictions that apply to corporate insiders. This requires the filing of various reports and the restriction of some trading activity, among other things. These issues are too technical for adequate discussion here. Public companies should consult with their legal counsel on these matters before designing a plan.

## Conclusion

Providing equity compensation for key employees, as you can see, involves a lot of competing choices. There is no one right or wrong formula. Corporate philosophy, fiduciary rules, the availability of stock and labor market issues, individual needs and warrants, and what the company has done in the past all bear on the ultimate decision. To make a good choice, it makes sense to talk with peers, look at surveys from your industry (but don't assume that because everyone else does it, that makes it a good strategy), get professional legal advice, and perhaps consult with a compensation advisor. Above all, don't get too locked in. Make sure your plans are flexible enough so that they can be changed to fit your changing circumstances.

# CHAPTER 2

# Compensating ESOP Company Executives in the New Regulatory and Accounting Environment

Alan A. Nadel and Virginia J. Bartlett

C ompensation planning for executives is no easy task. Changes brought about by new legislation, recent regulatory developments, and increased shareholder activity have significantly changed the landscape for compensation planners. Because of the greater levels of scrutiny existing today when compared to previous years, companies are becoming more vigilant in establishing relevant pay arrangements and setting appropriate compensation levels that effectively attract, retain, and motivate executives without "giving away the store" or otherwise being viewed as wasting corporate funds.

Some of these changes are noteworthy in their impact on both companies and executives. The tax laws have been changed so that arrangements that have the effect of deferring compensation are subject to onerous requirements. Many programs, including some that were not intended to defer compensation, have been swept up in the new rules, and companies are struggling to bring all of their compensation and benefits plans into compliance with the new guidelines.

This chapter looks at executive compensation in ESOP companies in light of recent legislative and regulatory changes, particularly new rules for deferred compensation, S corporation ESOPs, and new accounting requirements. It also discusses practical ways to provide appropriate executive compensation, particularly in closely held ESOP companies.

## Deferred Compensation Rules

The new (as of 2004) tax rules of Section 409A of the Internal Revenue Code (the "Code") are intended for any plan that has the effect of employees receiving compensation in a year later than the year in which their services were rendered. Although Section 409A is not intended for stock-based compensation per se, the very nature of equity compensation may lead some programs to fall under the new rules. The determination of which plans fall prey to Section 409A is made in a manner that is not necessarily intuitive and is determined differently than in other sections of the Code. For example, restricted stock and stock options usually vest in a year later than when they are granted and sometimes in a year later than when employee services are performed, yet generally they are not subject to Section 409A. On the other hand, options that are granted with any discount (i.e., where the exercise price is lower than value of underlying shares at date of grant) are fully subject to the rules of Section 409A, not just for the amount of the discount. Another anomaly is the grant of stock appreciation rights (SARs). Although SARs are economically equivalent to stock options, the Internal Revenue Service (IRS) treats them differently. The IRS has indicated that SARs are subject to Section 409A, with only a limited exception for certain SARs of publicly traded companies that are stock-settled.

Besides being broad in coverage, Section 409A significantly changes many of the accepted rules affecting deferred compensation and adds new ones as well. While the previous rules were based primarily on case law and IRS rulings, there is now a statutory framework governing any arrangement that defers compensatory payments. Some of the new rules are a continuation or variation of previous practice. Others add new burdens and layers of complexity for sponsoring companies, plus the risk of significant penalties for participating employees. Some of the highlights of Section 409A are:

- Elections to defer compensation generally must be made before the start of the taxable year in which the compensation is to be earned (or services performed).
- Deferral of performance-based compensation must be made at least six months before the end of the related service period. Per-

formance-based compensation is compensation that vests based on some corporate, group, or individual performance measurement. It does not refer to the grant of an award based on a performance measure.

- Changes in the timing of existing deferrals must fall within stated time frames and must result in an additional deferral of at least five years.

- Distributions of deferred payments may be made only under dates and circumstances specified in the plan or deferral agreement.

- Accelerated distributions of deferrals are severely curtailed.

- Certain payments to departing executives must be deferred for at least six months after termination.

- Funding though any sort of offshore trust is immediately taxable.

- The rules do not apply if the employee dies or becomes disabled, there is a change in control, or there is an unforeseen emergency (as rigorously defined in the law).

- The law does not apply to qualified benefit plans, such as ESOPs or 401(k) plans, as well as sick leave, death benefits, and similar arrangements. Existing rules for incentive stock options (incentive stock options are a specific kind of option subject to Section 422 of the Code) would not be changed by this law. Restricted stock would normally not be subject as well, but restricted stock units (restricted stock awards payable in stock when the awards vest) would be.

- Disclosures of all deferred amounts (whether or not currently taxable) must be made each year on Form W-2.

- Failure to comply with the new rules may result in significant penalties consisting of the accelerated tax amount, a 20% penalty tax, and an interest charge calculated at 1% over the IRS underpayment rate.

For example, say that a closely held company wants to reward its CFO with stock appreciation rights that vest three years after grant. Under the old rules, when the right vests, the executive might choose to defer the actual exercise of the award for an indefinite time, waiting until a strong valuation makes it appealing to act. Under the new rules, the CFO would have to decide to defer this exercise not later than the end of the year before the year in which vesting occurs (so if the award vests in 2009, the election would have to be made by December 31, 2007). Similarly, if the CFO wanted to defer the payment of cash from an incentive plan beyond when it would normally be paid, the decision would again have to be made not later than one year before the year in which the award normally would be paid. However, if the vesting in either case is based on, for example, the company hitting a sales target, the deferral election could be made up to six months before vesting.

In most cases, companies that maintain employee stock owner-ship plans (ESOPs) will be subject to Section 409A because they fre-quently use phantom equity plans, discounted stock options, certain stock appreciation rights, or other forms of equity compensation that fall under the new rules, as well as various kinds of deferred cash incen-tives. The new rules also are more restrictive for closely held compa-nies, which most ESOP companies are. For instance, all stock apprecia-tion rights issued after October 3, 2004, are considered deferred compensation in closely held companies, but SARs in public compa-nies meeting certain rules can be exempted from the rules (SARs issued before October 3, 2004, in closely held companies also can qualify if they were issued at fair market value, are not part of tandem awards, and contain no additional deferral features). This means that many equity-based plans must conform to the new rules tax rules for deferred compensation. Participating employees must make certain elections about the timing and form of payout from these plans, usually years in advance. Senior management employees may be unable to receive severance pay when they leave their companies but rather must wait for at least a six-month period. Other provisions of Section 409A also will apply, thereby inhibiting compensation planning for companies and employees alike.

## New Accounting Rules and Securities Law Issues

Another consideration is the Financial Accounting Standards Board's recently issued FAS 123R, which alters the approach most companies use to account for their stock-based compensation programs. ESOPs are specifically carved out from FAS 123R, but other equity-based corporate compensation plans fall under the new accounting rules. Certainly all public companies and many private ones are focused on their financial accounting and its effect on corporate earnings and balance sheets. The changes brought about by the new rules will adversely affect reported earnings in most cases and may influence the nature and types of equity programs that companies offer their employees.

A discussion of the new requirements of FAS 123R is beyond the scope of this chapter. In short, however, the new rules require that companies take a current charge against earnings for all equity compensation awards. To calculate the value of these awards, companies need to use a model, such as Black-Scholes or a lattice model, to calculate the fair market value of an award at grant.

To some extent, FAS 123R is not consistent with the newly enacted income tax rules of Section 409A. This may result in direct conflicts between the relevant accounting and income tax rules on substantive points, thereby making it more difficult for companies to establish compensation arrangements that effectively serve everyone's interests. An illustration of this conflict is the treatment of SARs. Stock appreciation rights become more attractive under FAS 123R than under the previous accounting rules because they will now be treated similarly to stock options. Presumably, companies would be inclined to use SARs in greater frequency because they have similar economics as options, are not as dilutive, do not require a detailed option valuation, soon will be accorded similar financial accounting treatment as options, and do not required employees to pay an exercise price. Because of the new tax rules of Section 409A, however, employees receiving SARs will be subject (in most cases) to additional requirements concerning deferral elections, timing of payments, potential penalties, and other tax issues not relevant to stock options. For instance, a company might issue 100 SARs to an employee at $100 per share in 2005, first exercisable in 2010. If the value rises to $175, the employee would be entitled to either $7,500 in cash or $7,500 worth of shares. The resulting dilution is only 75 shares if the SARS are settled in shares, but with options the dilution would have been 100 shares. Regardless of how the SARs are settled, the financial accounting treatment would be the same as for options. But the executive would have to decide in advance when to exercise the SARs, rather than being able to exercise them at a time when the price was optimal. Companies must weigh these inconsistencies in deciding how to compensate employees.

For public companies, the Securities and Exchange Commission (SEC) and the stock exchanges have imposed far-reaching rules that affect both the administration and disclosures concerning executive compensation. Of special concern are the new rules relating to equity compensation and how they affect public companies. Institutional shareholders and shareholder advocates have become more vocal about executive compensation, and employee groups, unions, and customers have joined the fray as well.

While private companies (ESOP or otherwise) are not the targets for many of these constituencies, increasingly they are becoming the focus of IRS and Department of Labor (DOL) attention. In the current environment, no one has an unfettered capability to freely set executive compensation levels without input and/or oversight from others. More so than at any other time in living memory, there is someone looking over the shoulders of those who set executive pay.

ESOP companies are subject to additional requirements under federal tax and labor laws. Key management employees in private companies often are the primary shareholders as well, and in many cases they serve as trustees of the ESOP. These key management employees in almost all cases control their own compensation to a great extent. The oversight of the SEC, institutional shareholders, and the media is not present in the case of a private company. Nor do the special rules of the stock exchanges apply.

## ERISA Issues

While not subject to securities laws applying to public companies, a private company that maintains an ESOP is subject to greater scrutiny by the IRS and DOL because there are more inherent conflicts for the ESOP company in setting compensation when compared to other private companies. Most private company executives also are shareholders and, consequently, any disagreements about compensation levels usually are quickly resolved. It is a matter addressed by the shareholders without the involvement of others. Where there is an ESOP, however, there is more potential for conflict and regulation. The IRS and DOL are concerned that even when there is an independent board of directors setting management pay, they are usually elected by those same managers who also serve as ESOP trustees.

Even if executives do not own much or any stock, they may still effectively set their own pay, even if they are not trustees. An independent ESOP trustee should focus on creating shareholder value for the participants in the ESOP, whereas the management team may be more focused on increasing cash flow for bonuses and salaries. The independent ESOP trustee in a privately held company will look at cash flow requirements with a view to increasing share values and satisfying the repurchase obligations of buying the ESOP stock from terminating ESOP participants first. Providing for additional salaries and bonuses for management employees can only be justified as an economically sustainable means to that end, not an end in itself.

The compensation-setting process also is more complicated for the ESOP company for a variety of other reasons than accounting, deferred compensation rules, and ERISA fiduciary requirements. As discussed below, the most important of these are rules that apply to an ESOP company that has elected to be taxed as an S corporation.

## Compensation Philosophy

The initial step in determining executive compensation is to examine the company's business strategy and to develop its overall approach to compensation. This ensures that the company's approach to compensating its executives is consistent with its overall business objectives and supports the company's business strategy. Establishing compensation programs that are in sync with the company's business objectives enables employees to engage in tasks that support those objectives and at the same time avoid activities that work against the company's interests. A well thought-out compensation philosophy should address basic issues such as fixed vs. variable pay, cash vs. equity compensation, and short-term vs. long-term compensation.

By making thoughtful choices about these issues as part of its approach to compensation, the company sets a foundation for whatever compensation arrangements it may establish in a manner that is consistent with its business objectives. This compensation philosophy sets the parameters that will drive any compensation arrangements the company chooses to implement for its employees, thereby ensuring programs that support the company's overall business strategy.

Once a company has identified its corporate business objectives and established a compensation philosophy, it must weigh other factors in designing specific arrangements for its executives and employees. Some of these considerations may be technical, while others may focus on business considerations that are specific to the company. These include:

- Performance motivation
- Performance evaluation
- Employee retention
- Financial security for employees
- Tax impact on company
- Tax effect to employees
- Financial statement impact
- Share dilution and overhang
- Disclosures to shareholders and other constituencies
- Other regulatory concerns

All of these issues (as well as others specific to the particular business) should be factored in when developing specific compensation and benefit programs.

## Reasonable Compensation

The issue of paying executives reasonable levels of compensation has become of great interest among public companies (and their constituents) in recent years. The press has been focusing considerable attention on executive pay, and we continue to hear a growing voice among shareholders and their advocates about this issue.

Primarily because of concerns about tax avoidance, the IRS has long focused on this issue in closely held companies. It is an issue that should be of interest for ESOP companies as well. The Department of Labor has started to take a special interest in officer compensation within ESOP companies. There have been a number of instances recently where the DOL examined officer compensation levels and questioned whether amounts paid to officers were excessive. This issue seems to be of greater concern where there are no other shareholders besides the ESOP and the officers in question. In closely held companies where key management employees often serve as ESOP trustees, it is advisable to have a group of independent members of the company's board of directors or an independent compensation consultant address salary and bonus issues. Using independent parties to establish the company's salary and bonus programs provides protection for the ESOP trustees if those programs are later challenged by the IRS, the DOL, or ESOP participants.

There are just two legal cases on this issue, perhaps indicating that while executive compensation is a concern, most ESOP companies have resolved this issue without ending up in court. These cases and their implications are discussed in detail in this book's chapter on fiduciary issues.

## Executive Compensation for ESOP Companies

There are few limitations on the ways that ESOP companies may compensate their executives, at least in how they differ from other companies. Cash compensation may be set at competitive market levels of pay or at whatever other levels that management (or the board of directors, if applicable) decides. Subject to prudent financial management, cash compensation may be tailored to fit each company's circumstances and its particular compensation philosophy.

Equity compensation is a different story. Unlike public companies and private companies that are not ESOP-owned, all ESOP companies must comply with myriad tax requirements. The rules for S corporation ESOP companies are even more restrictive. While private companies are not subject to the same ESOP financial accounting limitations as public companies are, the net result of the various tax rules is to limit the use by private companies of many stock-based programs, especially for S corporation ESOP companies. In C corporation ESOP companies, the primary concerns with equity compensation revolve around reasonableness, how sellers taking advantage of Section 1042 rollover rules acquire their ownership, and how to count various kinds of equity compensation when computing ownership levels for the purpose of the rules of Section 1042. While these issues are important, they are typically dealt with in the plan design stage and, as such, as beyond the scope of this chapter.

This is not to say that employees are prohibited from actual share ownership in ESOP companies. Companies maintaining C corporation tax status may grant restricted shares, phantom stock, SARs, stock options or other forms of equity or quasi-equity to their employees. Historically, because of the desire of private company owners to retain control of their organizations and maintain privacy, granting actual share ownership to employees has been more the exception than the rule. In some cases, this has been changing. While still relatively uncommon, outright grants of company equity have been used as a compensation tool in some ESOP companies. In many transactions, however, management is asked to purchase shares at fair market value to provide additional capital and/or appease lender wishes that members of management have "skin in the game."

To the extent compensation programs in ESOP companies are tied to stock, generally they take the form of stock options, phantom stock, restricted stock units (RSUs), and/or stock appreciation rights (SARs). Although each of these plans is denominated in the company's stock, in fact the employees typically receive only cash. In those cases the stock is used solely for measurement purposes, rather than for actual payment. With careful planning the company can base the program metrics on whatever stock values it deems appropriate. By using a consistent methodology for valuation of the company's shares, the company can develop a stock-based approach that is cash-denominated and does not produce unfavorable tax effects for participants. As discussed elsewhere, this approach may be of limited use for any individuals (or related parties) who own shares in a closely held S corporation with an ESOP because any grants, including phantom grants, may result in adverse tax effects.

The other alternative is to establish an incentive arrangement that is tied to performance criteria other than company stock. Using principles typically applied to bonus and incentive programs at other companies should result in a permitted incentive arrangement. Regarding S corporations (discussed in detail below), while the income tax regulations do not specify what is permitted, they caution against incentive arrangements that are intended to circumvent the single-class-of-stock requirements. This should give sufficient latitude to most S corporations to establish cash-based arrangements that address their specific business strategies and otherwise meet their needs without violating the single-class-of-stock requirements.

## Special Rules for S Corporations

Generally, the earnings of an S corporation are not taxed at the corporate level but rather are taxed to each of the shareholders. To the extent that any of the S corporation shareholders provide services through the company, they would be entitled to a salary or other compensation. Salary is tax-deductible in calculating the net earnings of the S corporation. Also, the company may pay bonuses or other forms of current compensation. Additionally, the salary and other compensation would be subject to both FICA and FUTA employment taxes. Any net earnings of the S corporation that still remain are passed through to the shareholders as dividends and are not subject to FICA or FUTA taxes.

In the case of an ESOP company that has elected S corporation status, the resulting pass-through effects can produce significant economic benefits to the company as well as to the ESOP. Because the ESOP is a tax-exempt entity, the corporate income that passes through the S corporation is not subject to taxation. The impact of corporate earnings accruing and compounding on a tax-exempt basis provides the company with more working capital and equity, which in turn results in lower financing costs and cheaper capital and, therefore, an ultimate higher value for the ESOP shares. All else being equal, participants in an S corporation ESOP will accrue greater levels of benefits than those who participated in an ESOP of a C corporation, albeit with an increase in the company's repurchase obligation to terminating ESOP participants.

## Second Class of Stock

One of the basic rules pertaining to S corporations is the prohibition on having more than one class of stock. This rule is based primarily on the rights to corporate distributions and liquidation proceeds. There are many techniques to compensate employees similarly to shareholders without having them deemed to be shareholders. Alternatively, employees could hold actual shares whose liquidation rights or voting rights would be materially different than those of other shares without being deemed to be a second class of a stock as a result of special exceptions applicable to individuals who are shareholder/employees (however, the ESOP must hold shares with the highest voting rights).

The most straightforward way of providing incentives to employees would be to provide bonuses based on corporate profitability. The income tax regulations generally view employee agreements as "not a binding agreement relating to distribution and liquidation proceeds" and thus not being a second class of stock unless a principal purpose of the agreement is to circumvent the single-class-of-stock rules. The regulations go on to say that, even if one shareholder's compensation is deemed to be excessive, that fact alone will not constitute a second class of stock, unless there was an intention to violate the single-class-of-stock rules. Similarly, call options issued to employees generally are not treated as constituting a second class of stock provided that they are not transferable and do not have a readily ascertainable fair market value at the time of issuance. While determining when options have a readily ascertainable fair market value is difficult, it generally occurs only if the options (not just the underlying shares) are publicly traded. Obtaining an appraisal for the value of company shares does *not* result in the related options having a readily ascertainable fair market value.

When a call option is granted at a discount to the stock's fair market value, however, the option may be viewed as constituting a second class of stock if the option is eventually materially modified or transferred to an ineligible shareholder. Essentially, this means that the company must issue options that are always nontransferable and have no readily ascertainable fair market value. Alternatively, the company could issue options that are transferable only to eligible shareholders and that have an exercise price at little or no discount to the fair market value of the underlying shares. The income tax regulations also indicate that companies may issue shares to employees and repurchase such shares at a discount without violating the single-class-of-stock rules. Agreements to repurchase the shares at death, divorce, disability, or other termination of employment are not considered in determining whether the shares confer identical rights to other company shares. Moreover, nonvested stock is treated as outstanding under the income tax regulations and forfeiture provisions relating to the shares are generally disregarded. Also, as previously noted, options issued at a discount likely will be subject to the new Section 409A rules for deferred compensation.

## S Corporation ESOPs

Until the mid-1990s, an ESOP was permitted to own shares only in a regular taxable C corporation. As a result of tax legislation that was enacted in 1996, it has become possible for S corporations to establish and maintain ESOPs. In addition to the general tax rules that are applicable to S corporations and the special rules that apply to ESOPs, there are additional legislative and regulatory requirements for S corporation ESOPs. The underlying tax rules were further modified in 2001, and again in 2004 and 2005, to prevent S corporation ESOPs from being abused in ways that provided benefits primarily to a small group of people, or even just one person. Inevitably, these rules made life more complicated for legitimate S corporation ESOP companies, requiring additional testing and, in some cases, changes in plan operations. Violation of any of the applicable rules may result in draconian taxation, including taxing the entire ESOP account balances of those individuals violating the maximum equity holdings rules as well as a 50% excise tax on the company and possible plan disqualification. Holders of synthetic equity outside the plan may also be taxed if their holdings violate the rules.

The universe of companies that can use S corporation ESOPs has diminished because of some of the limitations imposed by statute as well as by IRS regulations, but almost all of the companies excluded are those whose intentions were to use the tax benefits for only a small number of people. These abusive plans either had only a few employees to begin with or were structured so that a small management group (or even one manager) received most or all of the value of the tax benefits and/or equity in the company. The schemes devised to circumvent the law were very complicated and had little or no business purpose other than avoidance of the tax rules. Because dealing with these arrangements simply was difficult, the rules also effectively prohibit S corporation ESOPs in very small companies (typically 10–12 people or fewer). Legitimate ESOPs—those intended to broadly benefit plan participants—will not find that the rules prevent their being S corporation ESOPs, but may place some limits on the specific ways in which some employees may be compensated with equity.

The rules themselves are complicated, but they essentially state that ESOP companies must use a two-step process to determine whether the S corporation ESOP will not be subject to punitive tax treatment. First, companies must define "disqualified persons." Under the law, a "disqualified person" is an individual who has claims on 10% or more of the "deemed-owned" shares or who, together with family members (spouses or other family members, including lineal ancestors or descendants, siblings and their children, or the spouses of any of these other family members), has claims on 20% or more of the "deemed-owned" shares. "Deemed-owned" shares include allocations to the ESOP account of the person in question, a pro-rata allocation of unallocated ESOP shares, and any synthetic equity (broadly defined to include stock options, stock appreciation rights, and other equity equivalents).

Second, companies should determine whether disqualified individuals own at least 50% of all shares in the company. In making this determination, ownership is defined to include shares held directly, shares owned through synthetic equity, and allocated or unallocated shares owned through the ESOP.

If disqualified individuals own at least 50% of the stock of the company, they may not receive an allocation from the ESOP during that year without a substantial tax penalty. In 2004 and 2005, the IRS ruled that these disqualified individuals also may not accrue more than 10% of total ESOP allocations, or 20% for family members, without incurring a penalty. If such an allocation or accrual does occur, it is taxed as a distribution to the recipient, and a 50% corporate excise tax would apply to the fair market value of the stock allocated. If synthetic equity is owned, the 50% excise tax also would apply to its value as well. In the first year in which this rule applies, there is a 50% tax on the fair market value of shares allocated to or accrued by disqualified individuals even if no additional allocations are made to those individuals that year (in other words, the tax applies simply if disqualified individuals own more than 50% of the company in the first year). Complicated rules define just how to measure synthetic equity. These state, among other things, that any deferred compensation received more than 2½ years after award must be valued on an equity-equivalent basis. Additional rules describe in detail how to count various forms of ownership.

The extensive rules relating to S corporations with ESOPs, however, should not be interpreted to mean that executives may not receive incentive and deferred compensation. Provided that their awards do not result in a second class of stock and do not amount to so much synthetic equity that the limitations described above are exceeded, S corporations may provide most of the same kinds of awards any corporation would. The maximum ownership rules for S corporation ESOPs still allow individual executives to accumulate significant benefits without causing a violation. The limits are problematic mostly for executives who collectively or as families already own a large percentage of the company, such that their equity awards, ESOP allocations, and direct ownership total more than 50% of the total shares. Very small S corporation ESOP companies also may face more constraints, simply because key employees may have a large percentage of ESOP allocations as a result of the small number of total participants. By working with a qualified advisor, most companies that are not trying to use S corporation ESOP rules to focus benefits only on a small number of people should be able to find an array of solutions.

A different consideration arises, however, for S companies that are 100% owned by an ESOP. Because of their tax benefits, 100% S corporation ESOPs have become common and perhaps are the most common form of S corporation ESOP. In these companies, there is a compelling incentive not to structure distributions so participants ultimately own actual shares. The issue is that the ESOP must receive a pro rata share of any distributions made to owners. If the company made a distribution to someone owning, say, 5% of the stock as the result of option exercises, the ESOP would receive a distribution 19 times that amount, an impractical outcome. Stock appreciation rights, phantom stock, and cash-based incentive programs, whether short or long-term, make more sense.

## Reasonable Compensation

For the typical private company, the IRS often is focused on determining whether excessive levels of compensation have been paid to key employees. Because these individuals frequently are the shareholders, it is preferable from a tax standpoint to pay out corporate earnings in the form of compensation rather than as a dividend. Although both are taxable to the recipient, compensation is tax-deductible to the company, whereas dividends are not. In the typical audit of a private company, the IRS attempts to identify amounts claimed as compensation which in fact are dividends. Although this has no impact directly on the executive, it results in additional taxable income to the corporation.

The most common approach for avoiding any IRS claims of constructive dividends is the establishment of an S corporation. Because of its nature as a pass-through entity, the S corporation results in only one level of taxation, thereby thwarting any IRS attempts to reclassify compensation as dividends. Because there is little to be gained in terms of tax revenue, the IRS traditionally has not given its attention to S corporation officer compensation. Recently, however, the IRS has started to focus on S corporations and the issue of shareholder compensation (whether too high or too low) to identify what it perceives as abusive situations.

One reason for IRS concern relates to the issue of calculating retirement plan contributions. The company may contribute to a qualified retirement plan and receive a current income tax deduction to the extent that S corporation earnings are allocated to shareholder compensation. Net earnings of the S corporation that are not treated as compensation are instead treated as dividends and pass through directly to shareholders. As such, they are not eligible to serve as the basis for retirement plan contributions. The IRS has started to inquire about the determination of shareholder compensation.

In 2002 the U.S. Treasury issued a report that directed IRS attention to the determination of S corporation officer compensation. Rather than express concern about excessive officer compensation, the report suggested that S corporations frequently were paying insufficient amounts to executives. By not distributing corporate earnings as compensation (thereby treating such amounts as dividends), S corporations could avoid employment taxes on such amounts. There have been a number of recent cases in which S corporation shareholders withdrew "dividends," but the courts have usually indicated that such amounts are remuneration for services rendered and therefore must be treated as compensation.

There also have been tax cases that highlight the withdrawal of other amounts from S corporations as an attempt to avoid treatment as compensation. Special dividends, loans to shareholders and reimbursements for personal expenses have all been held by the courts to be forms of compensation. In 2003 there were six Tax Court cases that arrived at similar conclusions and established the following factors as considerations in determining whether officer compensation is sufficient:

- Officers perform substantial services for the S corporation.

- Officers receive distributions with respect to the stock .

- No other individuals work in the business.

- Most or all of the stock is owned by the officers.

- There are no loan documents for distributions that have been categorized as loans.

- S corporation officers have worked elsewhere in similar positions earning levels of pay that are significantly different than the amounts being reported as compensation by the S corporation.

- The company maintains no formula for determining annual salaries and bonuses.

- Compensation paid to the officers from the S corporation is at a rate less than compensation for similar positions at comparable companies.

- Officers are compensated at a rate less than nonshareholders who also manage the company.

No single factor will determine the treatment of S corporation distributions as shareholder compensation or otherwise. Instead, the courts have looked at the totality of the facts and circumstances in each case to determine the appropriate treatment for distributions to officers.

## Executive Compensation Issues for S Corporations with ESOPs

The determination of cash compensation for an S corporation with an ESOP is made using similar considerations as in other companies. Provided that cash is not being paid in a manner that is an end-run around the equity compensation limitations (see below), the company may set compensation at levels that it deems appropriate for its business.

Stock-based compensation is a different matter. As discussed elsewhere, granting restricted shares or stock options may be of limited use for individuals (or related parties) who already own shares in an S corporation ESOP company because any grants, including phantom grants, may result in taxable income for those individuals.

In some cases it will be possible to grant employees company shares (restricted or otherwise) or stock options on those shares. This is somewhat more complicated in the case of an S corporation because of the onerous S corporation rules that apply. For example, a basic requirement for any S corporation (ESOP-owned or otherwise) is the restriction of having only one class of stock, as previously discussed. If more than one class exists, the company may not avail itself of the benefits of being an S corporation, such as the pass-through of income. Generally, a stock option is not treated as a second class of stock if the option is deemed to be reasonable compensation, is nontransferable, and the option (not necessarily the shares) does not have a readily ascertainable fair market value.

Another issue is the outright grant of shares to an employee where the only exit strategy for the individual is to resell the shares back to the company. Generally, the purchase of employee-owned shares by the company does not violate the requirement for having a single class of stock, even when the shares are repurchased by the company at a bargain price upon the occurrence of certain events (e.g., before vesting).

Even in those cases where the single-class-of-stock rule is satisfied, the company must value the shares in most situations when employee shares or stock options are granted, vest or are repurchased by the company. The issue of share valuation presents some practical difficulties. The 2004 tax legislation brought extensive new rules dealing with deferred compensation. To the extent a nonqualified stock option is issued at less than fair market value (i.e., exercise price is less than fair market value at grant), the IRS guidelines indicate that the option grant is deemed to be deferred compensation and falls under the new tax rules of Section 409A. Likewise, the valuation of shares of restricted stock is also important in order to determine the amount of taxable income for employees (and deduction for the company) upon vesting (or grant, in the case of a Section 83(b) election). While many private companies took a relaxed attitude towards stock valuation in the past, the recent changes in Federal tax law have raised the risks of incorrect stock valuations.

The IRS has suggested that the valuation of private company shares by "completely independent and well-qualified experts . . . generally establishes that there was a good-faith attempt to meet the option price requirement." Whether other approaches will be recognized by the IRS remains unclear. In the past, many private companies valued their shares by referencing the values used in previous financings or by using industry or market-based rules of thumb about company values. It becomes less clear whether these approaches will work in light of the new tax rules of Section 409A. Furthermore, the costs, employee time, and business disruption associated with conducting stock valuations, possibly multiple times during the year, make this alternative unattractive for private companies. Even for ESOP companies where valuations are conducted at least annually for ESOP purposes, this approach is still troublesome because shares and stock options are not necessarily granted or vested at one or two specific dates during the year but rather at various dates throughout the fiscal year that are determined by other factors (e.g., the date of hire). A stock appraisal conducted many months ago may no longer be valid at the date of new equity grants. Thus, the alternative of granting restricted shares or stock options to senior employees may not be practical for many companies.

If an ESOP company finds the deferred compensation plan requirements under Section 409A or the special S corporation ESOP tax rules too restrictive or finds other tax rules affecting these plans unfavorable, a more feasible approach for may be to establish cash-based programs for executives and other senior employees, such as phantom stock, SARs, or performance units (a profit sharing formula based on longer-term profit goals). These may correlate directly or indirectly with the company's stock or may be based on other performance factors. As previously discussed, it will be important that any such plan be consistent with the company's business objectives and compensation philosophy (and structured so the grants do not constitute a second class of stock for S corporations).

## Conclusion

ESOP companies are more limited than other private companies in establishing executive compensation. Although stock-based programs generally are permitted, there are practical limitations to offering them in private companies, including ESOP companies. Where these rules seem too restrictive, a practical alternative for these employers is to establish cash-based incentive programs geared to their specific business strategies and compensation philosophy, thereby providing customization geared to specific corporate issues, employer flexibility, and compliance with the related income tax rules. In an ESOP company, it is advisable to use outside independent members of the company's board of directors or an independent compensation consultant to address the reasonableness of the company's compensation and bonus programs for management employees. The use of outside independent parties provides support if the compensation and benefit programs are later challenged by the IRS, DOL or ESOP participants.

# CHAPTER 3

# The 2005 NCEO Executive Compensation Survey

## Corey Rosen

In 2005, the NCEO sent an email message to approximately 1,000 ESOP companies asking them to provide detailed data on executive compensation practices through an online survey. We received 204 usable responses. All but two of the respondents were closely held companies. Respondents were asked to provide data on how executive compensation is set; the attributes of executive compensation; and the specific amounts for the CEO, COO, CFO, or other top financial officer, the top sales executive, the top divisional vice-president, and the top marketing, products, or service executive. For each of these categories, we asked respondents to tell us:

1. Cash compensation other than bonuses, profit sharing, or other incentive pay.

2. The estimated face value of deferred compensation granted in the last fiscal or calendar year as a percentage of base cash compensation.

3. The total percentage of stock represented by options, phantom stock, stock appreciation rights, or other contingent claims on future ownership of shares.

4. The percentage of total shares owned in the form of unvested restricted stock.

5.  The percentage of base cash compensation provided in the form of cash incentive pay in the last fiscal or calendar year.

6.  The total value of stock or stock rights granted in the last year as a percentage of cash compensation (counting restricted stock or phantom stock as $1 in stock = $1 in cash and counting stock options or stock appreciation rights as $3 in face value in options or SARs = $1 in cash).

In addition, we asked about how incentive compensation plans are structured, how executive compensation is determined, and what additional perquisites are provided.

Survey data on compensation can be very useful in determining appropriate levels of pay and benefits. But they also must be used with great caution. As your mother no doubt told you, "Just because everyone else is doing it doesn't mean you have to do it too." Each company's needs differ, and even the most detailed surveys cannot really provide many examples of companies just like yours. The survey reported here has a number of limits as well. While it is the only survey available looking at pay in ESOP companies, and while the response rate was much better than we anticipated, it is a national sample of a broad array of company sizes, industries, ownership situations, and other factors. This presentation looks only at the data overall. There are hundreds of ways the data can be "cut" (by size, industry, and percentage owned by the ESOP, for example, in multiple combinations) to narrow it down to companies that more precisely match your particular situation. The NCEO can provide a customized analysis in which a specific set of variables can be used to generate a report. Contact us for details about this service.

These caveats aside, there has long been an interest among ESOP companies in having data on compensation practices. While many good salary surveys are available from various industry and consulting sources, they include all kinds of companies. ESOP companies are very different in that part of executives' compensation comes from the ownership they have in the plan. In many cases, this is substantial, and account balances well into six figures are common for most executives with more than several years' seniority. Anecdotally, ESOP companies appear to take this into account when determining executive pay. So having a survey that focuses only on ESOP companies provides an important additional set of data.

## Sample Characteristics

There were 204 usable responses. The demographics of the companies are described in tables 3-1 and 3-2. Only one of the companies is publicly traded.

The sample is a reasonable reflection of ESOPs overall. For instance, the sample characteristics are almost identical to those in a somewhat larger survey we did in 2005 on how ESOP companies handle their repurchase obligations. Like ESOPs in general, the sample is

**Table 3-1. Plan Characteristics**

| Age of Plan | | % Owned by ESOP | | S or C | |
|---|---|---|---|---|---|
| Two years or less | 15.7% | 100% | 38.2% | S | 56.4% |
| Two to five years | 22.1% | 51%–99% | 23.0% | C | 43.6% |
| Five to ten years | 24.0% | 30%–49% | 27.0% | | |
| More than ten years | 38.2% | <30% | 11.8% | | |

**Table 3-2. Company Characteristics**

| Industry | | No. of Employees | | Change in Stock Value, Last Five Years | |
|---|---|---|---|---|---|
| Manufacturing | 21.7% | <100 | 47.5% | 20% or more | 15.8% |
| Retail | 6.4% | 100–500 | 39.2% | 10%–19% | 33.5% |
| Wholesale | 10.8% | 501–1,000 | 7.4% | 0%–10% | 37.9% |
| Insurance | 4.4% | >1,000 | 5.9% | <0% | 12.3% |
| Engineering/ architecture | 13.8% | | | | |
| Banking | 3.0% | | | | |
| Construction | 11.3% | | | | |
| Other services | 21.2% | | | | |
| Other | 7.4% | | | | |

dominated by small and mid-sized closely held companies with stronger than average stock performance over recent years. The sample also reconfirms the dramatic growth of 100% ESOP companies in recent years, something that was fairly rare until changes were made to S corporation rules in the late 1990s.

## Compensation Plan Attributes and Processes

One of the more contentious issues in the past few years for public companies has been how their boards set executive compensation. New stock exchange guidelines for independent board compensation committees, pressure from shareholders, and, indirectly, provisions of the Sarbanes-Oxley Act have all led more public companies to establish independent compensation committees to determine executive pay. Closely held companies, of course, are not held to the same standard. We asked respondents how they determined executive compensation. Table 3-3 displays the results. They are broken out by company size, as this would presumably play a major role in how active the board is.

As expected, the larger the company, the more the board relies on independent advice and/or has an independent committee.

**Table 3.3. How Executive Compensation Is Determined**

| Decision process | <100 employees | 100–500 employees | >500 employees |
|---|---|---|---|
| Board alone | 72.8% | 53.2% | 46.2% |
| Board with independent compensation advisor | 9.8% | 10.1% | 23.1% |
| Independent board compensation committee | 5.4% | 26.6% | 23.1% |
| Other | 12.0% | 10.1% | 7.7% |
| N | 97 | 80 | 27 |

## What Triggers Incentive Pay?

Of the 204 companies in the survey, 186 have some kind of incentive pay plan. Table 3-4 shows what triggers incentive pay: individual per-

**Table 3-4. What Triggers Incentive Pay***

| | |
|---|---|
| Individual targets | 34.8% |
| Department or division targets | 27.9% |
| Corporate profit | 74.0% |
| Change in stock price | 8.8% |

*Companies can indicate more than one response.
N = 204

formance, department or division targets, corporate profit, a change in stock price, or something else. Company size does not make a difference here, so there is no breakdown by size.

In recent years, shareholders have pushed companies to require that performance targets be met before incentive awards, including equity awards, vest. Ninety-two percent of the respondents do not subject cash incentive awards to vesting. Among stock awards, 36% are not subject to vesting at all, while just 2.5% are subject to performance vesting. The rest vest over time, with the largest group vesting in four to five years.

# Types of Awards

Executive compensation can have several features, including deferred compensation, stock options and similar plans, restricted stock, incentive compensation, and perquisites. A striking result of the survey is that relatively few companies—just 51 of the 204 respondents—use stock awards, including stock options, stock appreciation rights, phantom stock, and restricted stock. Restricted stock is used by very few companies. The tendency to use stock options, phantom stock, or stock appreciation rights varies with the percentage of ownership, as table 3-5 indicates. Company size, however, is not a significant differentiator. (The next section of this chapter discusses award size.)

Of all corporate officers, CEOs are the most likely to receive equity awards: 17% of them receive options, phantom stock, or SARs. Among those 17% of CEOs, equity awards represent approximately 11% of the total shares of company stock. Among other corporate officers, between 10% and 14% receive equity awards, representing between 4

**Table 3-5. Use of Stock Options, Phantom Stock, and Stock Appreciation Rights for CEOs, by Percentage of Ownership**

| % ESOP ownership | % of Companies Using | Value of Most Recent Award as % of Pay* |
|---|---|---|
| <50% | 11.4% | 21.3% |
| 51%-99% | 23.4% | 29.3% |
| 100% | 19.5% | 36.9% |

*Calculated by assessing the face value of phantom stock as a percentage of the most recent cash compensation and one-third the value of stock options or stock appreciation rights as a percentage of the most recent compensation.

and 6% of company stock. All equity awards, including stock, represent a value equivalent to 18% to 50% of base cash compensation, depending on the officer.

Aside from cash compensation, many companies offer various perquisites to executives, as described in tables 3-6 through 3-8. *Note: In tables 3-6 through 3-8, companies that did not respond to the survey item were classified as not offering the perquisites.*

Tables 3-7 and 3-8 show that size does not affect the types of perquisites offered, with the exception of top-hat retirement plans, which are more common in larger companies. The question did not ask companies to estimate the value of the perquisites, however. Only life insurance and disability insurance are commonly offered benefits.

## Cash, Deferred, and Incentive Compensation Averages

Tables 3-9 through 3-11 look at how much executives were paid in cash, deferred, and incentive compensation other than options or other equity awards. The amounts do not include equity awards, although, as noted above, such awards are not used in the majority of companies. The totals are broken out by company size for fewer than and more than 100 employees.

Table 3-9 shows the average base cash compensation for CEOs, COOs, top financial/accounting executives, top sales/marketing executives, top manufacturing/products/services VPs, and top divisional VPs. The results are broken down by company size.

Table 3-6. Perquisites Offered to Top Executives*

|  | CEOs | Other Executives |
|---|---|---|
| Top-hat retirement plans | 5.4% | 4.4% |
| Life insurance | 51.5% | 41.2% |
| Personal travel/transportation | 28.4% | 20.1% |
| Entertainment | 16.7% | 13.2% |
| Disability | 42.6% | 38.2% |
| Other | 14.7% | 11.3% |

*Companies can choose more than one response.
$N = 204$

Table 3-7. Perquisites Offered to CEOs, by Company Size

|  | <100 employees | 100–500 employees | >500 employees |
|---|---|---|---|
| Top-hat retirement plans | 2.1% | 8.8% | 7.4% |
| Life insurance | 55.7% | 48.8% | 44.4% |
| Personal travel/transportation | 26.8% | 28.8% | 33.3% |
| Entertainment | 17.5% | 15.0% | 18.5% |
| Disability | 45.4% | 37.5% | 48.1% |
| Other | 10.3% | 18.8% | 18.5% |
| N | 97 | 80 | 27 |

Table 3-8. Perquisites Offered to Non-CEO Top Executives, by Company Size

|  | <100 employees | 100–500 employees | >500 employees |
|---|---|---|---|
| Top-hat retirement plans | 1.0% | 7.5% | 7.4% |
| Life insurance | 40.2% | 42.5% | 40.7% |
| Personal travel/transportation | 16.5% | 22.5% | 25.9% |
| Entertainment | 12.4% | 13.8% | 14.8% |
| Disability | 37.1% | 37.5% | 44.4% |
| Other | 7.2% | 15.0% | 14.8% |
| N | 97 | 80 | 27 |

**Table 3-9. Mean Base Cash Compensation, All Companies**

| Base Cash Compensation | 100 Employees or Fewer | Over 100 Employees |
|---|---|---|
| CEO/president | $175,524 | $238,830 |
| COO | $129,626 | $180,873 |
| Top financial/accounting executive | $86,837 | $130,251 |
| Top sales/marketing executive | $112,349 | $133,954 |
| Top mfg/products/services VP | $104,115 | $123,491 |
| Top divisional VP | $111,495 | $134,297 |

Table 3-10 covers results *only for those companies that report an active deferred compensation plan.* For example, 26% of companies with 100 or fewer employees offer deferred compensation to their CEOs. CEOs in those companies have a base cash compensation of $152,369, and the average size of the deferred compensation award in those companies is equivalent to 27% of the CEO's base cash compensation.

Table 3-11 covers results *only for those companies that report an active incentive compensation plan.* For example, 63% of companies with over 100 employees offer incentive compensation to their CEOs. CEOs in those companies have a base cash compensation of $255,689, and the average size of the incentive compensation award in those companies is equivalent to 44% of the CEO's base cash compensation.

The data indicate that while cash compensation is king at most companies, incentive pay can be a significant addition at more than half of the companies. Deferred compensation plays a less significant role. There are, of course, many ways to look at the data, only one of which is presented here. As noted above, the NCEO can provide the detailed data from the survey based on selected parameters so that users can look at each individual response as well as compute means and medians. The data do not, however, allow for the identification of individual company identities, nor are the responses specific enough as to size, percentage of ESOP ownership, and industry to allow a good guess.

How do these data compare to other data on executive compensation? The most comparable large data set we could locate comes from CompData Surveys. These data are not precisely comparable. The

Table 3-10. Mean Compensation for Companies with Deferred Compensation

| | 100 or Fewer Employees | Over 100 Employees |
|---|---|---|
| **CEO/President** | | |
| % of companies offering deferred compensation to CEO | 26% | 40% |
| Base cash compensation for CEOs with deferred compensation | $152,369 | $243,813 |
| Deferred CEO compensation (as a percentage of base cash compensation) | 27% | 36% |
| **COO** | | |
| % of companies offering deferred compensation to COO | 7%* | 20% |
| Base cash compensation for COOs with deferred compensation | $145,382* | $180,640 |
| Deferred COO compensation (as a percentage of base cash compensation) | 73%* | 22% |
| **Top Finance/Accounting Executive** | | |
| % of companies offering deferred compensation to CFO | 15% | 36% |
| Base cash compensation for CFOs with deferred compensation | $85,395 | $132,068 |
| Deferred CFO compensation (as a percentage of base cash compensation) | 21% | 22% |
| **Top Sales/Marketing Executive** | | |
| % of companies offering deferred compensation to sales/mktg exec | 13% | 27% |
| Base cash compensation for sales/mktg exec with deferred compensation | $106,506 | $140,685 |
| Deferred sales/mktg exec compensation (as a percentage of base cash compensation) | 41% | 25% |
| **Top Mfg/Products/Services VP** | | |
| % of companies offering deferred compensation to mfg/prod/svc VP | 12% | 19% |
| Base cash compensation for mfg/prod/svc VP with deferred compensation | $87,045 | $120,613 |
| Deferred mfg/prod/svc VP compensation (as a percentage of base cash compensation) | 24% | 19% |
| **Top Divisional VP** | | |
| % of companies offering deferred compensation to divisional VP | 10% | 21% |
| Base cash compensation for divisional VP with deferred compensation | $102,814 | $142,069 |
| Deferred divisional VP compensation (as a percentage of base cash compensation) | 14% | 26% |

* Few small-company COOs receive deferred compensation, so these numbers should be viewed with extreme caution.

**Table 3-11. Mean Compensation for Companies with Incentive Compensation**

|  | 100 or Fewer Employees | Over 100 Employees |
|---|---|---|
| **CEO/President** | | |
| % of companies offering incentive compensation to CEO | 43% | 63% |
| Base cash compensation for CEOs with incentive compensation | $168,318 | $255,689 |
| Incentive CEO compensation (as a percentage of base cash compensation) | 42% | 44% |
| **COO** | | |
| % of companies offering incentive compensation to COO | 16% | 29% |
| Base cash compensation for COOs with incentive compensation | $143,726 | $191,488 |
| Incentive COO compensation (as a percentage of base cash compensation) | 33% | 40% |
| **Top Finance/Accounting Executive** | | |
| % of companies offering incentive compensation to CFO | 31% | 59% |
| Base cash compensation for CFOs with incentive compensation | $95,607 | $143,230 |
| Incentive CFO compensation (as a percentage of base cash compensation) | 23% | 30% |
| **Top Sales/Marketing Executive** | | |
| % of companies offering incentive compensation to sales/mktg exec | 29% | 49% |
| Base cash compensation for sales/mktg exec with incentive compensation | $105,024 | $141,150 |
| Incentive sales/mktg exec compensation (as a percentage of base cash compensation) | 30% | 30% |
| **Top Mfg/Products/Services VP** | | |
| % of companies offering incentive compensation to mfg/prod/svc VP | 22% | 35% |
| Base cash compensation for mfg/prod/svc VP with incentive compensation | $110,839 | $130,988 |
| Incentive mfg/prod/svc VP compensation (as a percentage of base cash compensation) | 26% | 30% |
| **Top Divisional VP** | | |
| % of companies offering incentive compensation to divisional VP | 19% | 37% |
| Base cash compensation for divisional VP with incentive compensation | $114,383 | $144,397 |
| Incentive divisional VP compensation (as a percentage of base cash compensation) | 27% | 37% |

CompData survey provides annual cash compensation for companies with employee populations using measurements similar to ours, but they break down incentive pay only by revenues. They also have different assumptions about how pay, such as options, is counted. Tables 3-12 and 3-13 make some simplifying assumptions to come up with very roughly comparable numbers, but the CompData comparison points may be off by a factor of about 10% to 20%. No mater how they are looked at though, the key point is that ESOP company executives do not make nearly as much as comparable non-ESOP company executives.

**Table 3-12. Total Compensation, NCEO vs. CompData National Sample**
*Up to 100 Employees*

|  | NCEO Survey | CompData |
|---|---|---|
| CEO | $210,923 | $380,000 |
| COO | $150,297 | $218,000 |
| CFO | $99,544 | $142,000 |
| Top sales/mktg exec | $126,211 | $178,000 |

**Table 3-13. Total Compensation, NCEO vs. CompData National Sample**
*More Than 100 Employees*

|  | NCEO Survey | CompData |
|---|---|---|
| CEO | $329,905 | $438,000 |
| COO | $226,332 | $285,00 |
| CFO | $163,983 | $163,000 |
| Top sales/mktg exec | $177,803 | $202,000 |

This comparison is admittedly a very rough one. There may be systematic variations in the kinds of businesses represented in the two surveys, for instance, and the calculations here are not precisely apples-to-apples. They are, however, consistent with what many ESOP advisors say: cash compensation for ESOP executives is somewhat below market. On the other hand, these ESOP executives are often substantial participants in the ESOP and, as noted, often can look forward to six-figure or higher account balances, an asset that few non-ESOP executives would have.

## Conclusion

It is important to emphasize again that these data, while providing ballpark figures, should not be used as precise yardsticks for setting executive pay. As the other chapters in this book point out, even the most precisely comparable surveys should be used with considerable caution. Nonetheless, these data provide useful additional information for companies in seeking to determine appropriate levels of executive compensation.

*To order a custom report based on this survey or to acquire the entire data set for your own analyses, see the back of this book.*

# CHAPTER 4

# Using Competitive Compensation Studies at ESOP Companies

## Helen H. Morrison and Christine Robovsky

T he recent spate of corporate financial and governance scandals—
Enron, Worldcom, and Tyco, to name just a few—have led to
increased media attention and public awareness of the level and
form of executives' compensation. Initially, legislation and regulations
addressing executive compensation were focused exclusively on public companies. For example, Sarbanes-Oxley limits the form and timing of payments to public company executives. Also, the NYSE and
NASDAQ adopted rules that require a shareholder vote on certain types
of executive compensation programs.

More recent laws, regulations, and enforcement initiatives that
address excessive and noncompliant forms of management compensation are targeted at private as well as public companies. For example,
Congress recently added a provision to the Internal Revenue Code that
governs nonqualified deferred compensation (Section 409A). FASB's
stock option expensing rules (FAS 123R), which are an outgrowth of
increased attention on management compensation programs, are applicable to all companies beginning in 2006. Additionally, the IRS has
undertaken an executive compensation audit initiative, which is targeted at larger companies but makes no distinction between public
and private companies.

Scrutiny of management's compensation is not a new concept for
ESOP-owned companies. ESOP fiduciaries have been sued in two

cases—*Delta Star, Inc. v. Patton,* 76 F. Supp. 2d 617 (W.D. Pa. 1999) and *Eckelkamp v. Best,* 315 F.3d 863 (8th Cir. 2002)—on the grounds that the value of the company stock price suffered because the executives received "excessive" compensation. In *Delta Star,* the ESOP participants prevailed based, in part, on the fact that the company's president (who also acted as the ESOP trustee) unilaterally granted himself salary increases, bonuses, and nonqualified retirement benefits without consulting the company's other board members or outside consultants regarding industry standards or the proper criteria to be used to establish his compensation. In *Eckelkamp,* the ESOP trustee prevailed thanks, in part, to a compensation structure that the court found to be well-documented and well-designed. Management's compensation was found to be competitive with the industry, reflective of company performance, and aligned with the interest of employee and other shareholders. These cases support the need to support and document the levels and forms of compensation provided to an ESOP company's management team.

Due to the heightened attention given management compensation, ESOP companies and ESOP fiduciaries are advised to give particular consideration to the compensation packages of key management employees.

This chapter addresses how a competitive compensation study can assist ESOP-owned companies in establishing the appropriate level of compensation for the management team and designing annual and long-term incentive compensation programs that promote (rather than dilute) shareholder value. The chapter explains what a competitive compensation study is, how it is done, and how it is used most effectively by ESOP-owned companies.

The focus here is on management compensation. The use of competitive compensation studies of nonmanagement employees is beyond the scope of this chapter.

## What Is a Competitive Compensation Study, and Why Should You Do One?

A competitive compensation study provides data to assist the employer to assess whether its pay programs are competitive and consistent with its compensation philosophy. Competitive compensation studies take on many forms. They may range from informal surveys of known competitors or other employers of similar size in the same geographic area to formal analyses completed by an outside compensation consultant.

Competitive compensation studies can be used in a number of ways. The most obvious purpose of a study is to determine whether the individuals in the top management group are compensated at a competitive level. The study also can be used to assist with designing the allocation of base compensation, annual bonuses, and long-term incentives in the compensation mix, and to determine the level of awards to be granted under the long-term incentive plan. Additionally, a compensation study can be used to determine the proper level of compensation to offer to new executives or to retain existing executives.

In ESOP-owned companies, the level of management compensation is an important factor in determining share value. Consequently, the board of directors, compensation committee, or senior management of an ESOP-owned company may engage a compensation study to be performed to provide the ESOP trustee and its financial advisor with information about how the company's management compensation compares to that of its peer group and companies of a similar size and in a similar industry.

The objective of any competitive compensation study is to compile "market pricing" data. How this data is used, however, depends on the employer's circumstances and the purpose for undertaking the analysis. It must be emphasized that competitive compensation analysis is not an exact science. As discussed in greater detail below, a compensation study is merely the starting point for determining the appropriate levels and forms of management compensation. Whether the purpose of the study is to determine the proper compensation level for a particular person or position or to design an appropriate incentive compensation plan, the employer must always consider its unique circumstances, market conditions, and other applicable factors.

## How Is a Competitive Compensation Study Done?

Although a compensation study may be done on an informal basis using internal resources, a formalized study completed by a third-party consultant has certain benefits. The consultant brings expertise to determine the parameters of the analysis, compile and interpret the data, and provide recommendations based on market experience and financial, accounting, and tax expertise. Of course, working with an outside consultant requires a larger budget for the project.

For the purpose of this section, we assume that the employer has elected to undertake a formal competitive compensation study with an outside consultant. We will address the steps in the process and highlight issues of particular interest to ESOP-owned companies.

## Defining Objectives

A competitive compensation analysis generally begins by defining the employer's objectives for the study. To develop an understanding of the objectives, the employer should be prepared to respond to the following questions:

- What are the number of positions and individuals to be reviewed?

- Will the study consider only cash compensation (base salary and annual bonus) or total compensation (base salary, annual bonus, and long-term incentive compensation)?

- Will the study be used as a basis to design a long-term incentive compensation program and to determine the level of awards to be made under the program?

## Understanding the Employer's Compensation Philosophy and Policies

The next step in the process requires an understanding of the employer's compensation philosophy and policies. Some of the issues discussed with the employer as part of this step include:

- the criteria for identifying competitors (e.g., industry type, organization size, or geographic location);

- the target market position for management compensation levels (the 25th percentile, 50th percentile (median), or 75th percentile);

- the desired mix of pay (e.g., fixed vs. at-risk compensation, or short term vs. long-term incentives);

- constraints on annual cash cost of compensation programs and annual accounting expense; and

- the relative importance of various incentive considerations such as retention, rewarding specific goal achievement, linking compensation to stock price performance, or tax effects on the employee and employer.

## Selection of Surveys and Identification of Publicly Traded Peer Group

The consultant will identify the compensation surveys that fit with the employer's objectives for the study and its compensation philosophy. Certain surveys are publicly available, while others are proprietary and may be used only if the employer participated in the survey. Whatever survey data is used, it is important that it is a good match for the company. For example, if the employer is a healthcare company with $500 million in revenue, the surveys that are used should be able to be tailored to the healthcare industry and able to be broken down to a $500 million revenue size.

The consultant must also assess whether the survey sponsor is reputable and the date is reliable. Additional questions that will be considered as part of this analysis are whether the survey job descriptions are adequate for good job matching, how large the survey is, and whether a sufficient number of the client's market competitors participate in the survey to make it a reliable resource.

Survey data is not collected and compiled consistently. For example, some surveys report the data by taking an average compensation (the "mean") of all employees represented in the particular job category. In this case, if one company had a large number of employees in the sample, its data could overly influence the statistics. Other surveys consider the data on a company-by-company basis and provide a "weighted mean," which is the average of all employees considered, and also the "mean," which is the company mean. Also, a large difference between mean and median statistics can be the result of a sample that is skewed high or low by a few unusual cases. It is the responsibility of the consultant to properly interpret the data provided by the various surveys.

The consultant will also work with the employer to identify comparable publicly traded companies. For private ESOP-owned business, this process is relatively easy because the companies that will be included in the list are generally those that are used by the ESOP trustee's financial advisor for the purpose of valuing the business. These public companies are used for the purpose of compensation comparison for the CEO and any other similarly situated officers whose compensation is disclosed in the comparable companies' public filings.

### Job "Benchmarking"

A critical step in the analysis is to properly match the internal positions that are being analyzed (referred to as the "benchmark" jobs) to the job descriptions in the survey sources. Benchmark matches should be based on job content in comparison with the survey's job description. Additional information that will be considered includes the title, internal reporting structure, and position within the organizational hierarchy. As a guideline, if 70% or more of the job content is comparable, it is generally considered a strong match. The individual whose position is being analyzed is often referred to as the "incumbent."

At times, the incumbent in the benchmark job may have a combination of duties. For example, the CFO of the organization may also be responsible for the human resources function. If this is the case, the consultant will work with the employer to determine whether it is appropriate to apply an adjustment factor to the survey compensation numbers (e.g., a 15% increase) to adjust for the fact that the individual in that position has greater experience and more responsibilities that the survey job descriptions. Such an adjustment should be used judiciously because it leaves the objectivity of the analysis open to challenge.

### Data Analysis

The analysis of the compensation data is generally divided into three parts: (1) base salary; (2) total cash compensation (TCC), which includes base compensation and annual bonus; and (3) total direct compensation (TDC), which includes base compensation, annual bonus and long-term incentives.

### Base Salary and Total Cash Compensation Data Analysis

After determining the appropriate position matches from each survey source, the following methodology is applied to determine compensation competitiveness of base salary and TCC:

- Data is collected on base salary and TCC at the 25th, 50th (median), and 75th percentiles from each of the identified surveys.

- The compensation data for each position is statistically adjusted using a regression analysis that adjusts the compensation data to a level related to the incumbent's actual revenue responsibility at the company. (A regression analysis is a statistical calculation that analyzes the relationship between two variables. In compensation analyses, a regression analysis is used to measure the relationship between compensation and revenue or some other factor that strongly indicates the scope of the position, such as the number of full-time employees.) For example, an employer has four vice presidents of regional sales whose positions are being considered. Although the job description for these positions is identical, the revenue responsibility may vary dramatically. The regression analysis will adjust the competitive compensation results to account for the difference in revenue responsibility.

- If the industry-specific data is not sufficient to permit a valid regression analysis (at least 10 companies in the survey), a larger data pool will be used (e.g., general industry data).

- For competitive compensation analysis of senior officers of the employer, the compensation data compiled generally will be based on national data on the assumption that senior management are highly mobile and often recruited on a national basis.

- The survey date will be "aged" to a common effective date using an acceptable annual increase factor.

- Finally, competitive base salary and TCC is collected from the most recently filed proxy statements of the employer's comparable public companies.

### Long-Term Incentive and Total Direct Compensation Data Analysis

Analysis of competitive long-term incentive (LTI) compensation is often the most difficult part of the analysis. Unlike cash compensation, LTI can take the form of restricted stock grants, stock options, stock appreciation rights (SARs), phantom shares, or performance units. These LTI awards are more challenging to value. In addition, LTI awards are not always made on an equal annual basis. Instead, large grants subject to a vesting schedule may be made every three or more years.

These difficulties are overcome by using an option pricing model (such as Black-Scholes) to value the stock options and SARs, fair market value to value the restricted stock, and the target value to value the cash-based long-term incentives. In addition, it is typical to apply a three-year average for LTI grants to smooth out uneven long-term incentive grant patterns.

Certain surveys publish LTI data exclusively for privately held companies. Other surveys include all companies (public and private) in a particularly industry. The LTI value in these surveys is typically expressed as a multiple of base salary. This value is then compared to the benchmark positions' competitive compensation for base salary at the 25%, 50% (median), and 75% percentile levels to determine the competitive LTI dollar values.

### Delivery of the Report

Upon completion of the data compilation and analysis, the employer will receive a report that graphically shows for each benchmark position the TCC (total cash compensation), LTI (long-term incentive), and TDC (total direct compensation, which includes TCC and LTI) as compared to the 25th, 50th (median), and 75th percentiles.

## How Do ESOP Companies Use Competitive Compensation Studies?

For the most part, ESOP-owned companies are no different than other employers who have the desire to assess the competitiveness of their management compensation programs. It is important for any employer that undertakes a competitive compensation study to understand that the study is only the starting point in determining pay levels. Other factors must be considered, such as the employee's experience, institutional knowledge, leadership skills, tenure, industry experience, marketing skills, and job performance, along with the perceived risk that the employee may leave the company and the associated replacement costs. The employer must also consider its own competitive and marketplace circumstances.

ESOP-owned companies do have some unique considerations. To begin with the employer maintains an ESOP. In many cases, the annual ESOP benefit provided to employees may be well above market for retirement plan benefits. We are often asked whether the ESOP should be included in the LTI analysis for management compensation. Our answer is an emphatic negative. The ESOP is clearly a retirement plan and should be treated as such and not included as part of the LTI or any other part of the compensation analysis. Having said this, the ESOP benefit is clearly a factor that an ESOP employer should consider in setting its compensation philosophy and determining the appropriate level of competitive compensation.

ESOP companies also have a unique fiduciary obligation to the employee/ESOP participants. This obligation makes it particularly important to assure that management's compensation is at a reasonable and competitive level, and that the forms of annual bonus and LTI are appropriate to motivate the management team to grow the share value.

For many ESOP companies, particularly S corporation ESOP-owned companies, the tax rules limit the type of LTI plans that may be established for the benefit of the management team. A detailed discussion of the proper forms of LTI compensation for ESOP-owned companies is beyond the scope of this chapter. However, an important use of any competitive compensation study is to assist the employer to design a practical LTI plan and determine the appropriate award levels under that plan to properly compensate the management team and also promote the growth in shareholder value.

## Conclusion

Competitive compensation studies may be used effectively by ESOP-owned companies to assure they are compensating the management group at a level that is competitive and consistent with industry standards. Good corporate governance for all companies, including ESOP-owned companies, requires the board of directors (and its compensation committee) to assure that the executives are compensated fairly, but not to excess. In an ESOP-owned company, the ESOP fiduciaries, which include the ESOP committee and ESOP trustee, have an obligation to understand the management group's compensation. They should assess whether the level of compensation is consistent with competitive standards. Equally important, they should consider whether the short-term and long-term compensation incentives provide the management group with the proper motivation to grow the value of the business. A well-constructed compensation study helps the board of directors, the compensation committee, and the ESOP fiduciaries to make all of these determinations.

# CHAPTER 5

# Fiduciary Issues for ESOP Trustees Regarding Executive Compensation

Marilyn H. Marchetti, James E. Staruck, and Julie A. Williams

E mployee stock ownership plan (ESOP) trustees often examine issues involving executive compensation, which can take many forms. Executive compensation includes not only the executive's salary and bonus but also synthetic equity such as stock options, stock appreciation rights (SARs), and phantom stock; additional compensation plans such as a supplemental executive retirement plan (SERP); benefits triggered upon a change of control; and various transaction bonuses. This chapter addresses the role of the ESOP trustee in its consideration of executive compensation.

## Overview

An ESOP trustee is not required to automatically object to any award to executives of cash bonuses or synthetic equity, such as options, SARs, or any of the other forms of executive compensation referenced above. These compensation arrangements have proven to be excellent ways of attracting, retaining, and rewarding top-quality management. In fact, it is often in the best interest of an ESOP trustee to encourage these types of incentives to align the interests of the management team with that of the shareholders. The issue that faces ESOP trustees arises where executive compensation is excessive relative to market standards and, therefore, has an unfairly dilutive impact on the value of the shares held in the ESOP.

The Employee Retirement Income Security Act of 1974 (ERISA) provides that an ESOP trustee must discharge its duties with respect to the ESOP solely in the interests of plan participants and for the exclusive purpose of providing benefits to participants and their beneficiaries.[1] The case law that has expanded upon this concept provides that an ESOP trustee has an unwavering duty to make decisions with a single-minded devotion to ESOP participants.[2] Furthermore, if an ESOP trustee knows that executive compensation is excessive and unfairly dilutive to the ESOP, the trustee has an obligation to take action to carry out its duties under ERISA.

## Case Law

Case law provides some guidance on the duty of an ESOP trustee when executive compensation is excessive. There are two leading cases relevant to this issue: *Delta Star, Inc. v. Patton*[3] and *Eckelkamp v. Beste*.[4]

### The *Delta Star* Case

In *Delta Star*, Andrew Patton was one of the co-trustees of the Delta Star ESOP. He was also Delta Star's chairman and vice president. The other trustees were Christian Pany and James Austin. The ESOP owned 98.63% of the stock, and key management members, including Patton, Pany, and Austin, owned the remaining 1.37%. Patton, Pany, and Austin, as trustees of the ESOP, elected themselves as sole members of the board of directors. In the years following the implementation of the ESOP, Delta Star's financial performance was very cyclical due to the nature of the industrial transformer industry within which it operated. However, even in years when sales spiked, the company's net income remained flat because of the excessive salary increases and bonuses that Patton caused to be paid out to members of management, in particular to himself. For example, in one year, Patton declared a bonus for himself equal to $1.04 million, or approximately 400% of his base salary, even though the average bonus for a CEO in Delta Star's industry was 39% of base salary. Further, his bonuses typically exceeded the amounts that were allowable under Delta Star's credit agreement with its lender. He never obtained board approval for any of these increases or bonuses. In addition, Patton's compensation package was above the 75th percentile of compensation paid to other CEOs in the industry, even though the comparable companies were much larger than Delta Star. Also, because the contributions that could be allocated to Patton in the ESOP were limited by the applicable provisions of ERISA and the Internal Revenue Code, Patton directed that he be awarded with a SERP and other related benefits to make up for what he would have received had those limitations not been in place. The formula for determining amounts to be awarded under these plans was much more aggressive than the formula that is typically used. Once Patton retired and new members of the board of directors were appointed, they initiated a suit against him in his capacity as a board member for breaching his fiduciary duty to the shareholders as well as in his capacity as an ESOP trustee for breaching his fiduciary duty to the ESOP participants.

The court found that the compensation paid to Patton was excessive, unreasonable, and diminished the value of the stock held in the ESOP. The court held that Patton, in his capacity as an ESOP trustee, breached his fiduciary duty to the ESOP participants by voting the ESOP shares in favor of his retention as a member of the Delta Star board and by failing to take action as an ESOP trustee to remove himself from the board of directors or otherwise prevent the excessive and unreasonable compensation that was paid to him. The court noted that an ESOP trustee has a duty to avoid placing himself in a position where his acts as an officer or director will prevent his ability to function with complete loyalty to the ESOP participants. The court also held that an ESOP trustee has a duty to bring a derivative action if it is aware that officers and/or directors have breached the fiduciary duties that they owe to the shareholders of the company.

## The *Eckelkamp* Case

The *Eckelkamp* case contrasts with the *Delta Star* case. In this case, as in *Delta Star*, the ESOP trustees were insiders of the Melton Machine and Control Company ESOP. However, unlike in *Delta Star*, following the inception of the ESOP, the average rate of return on the stock was 20% per year. The court found that a substantial part of this increase was due to the changes that management, particularly the individuals who also were the ESOP trustees, had implemented in an effort to increase sales and improve margins. Nevertheless, the plaintiffs, who were ESOP participants, contended that the ESOP trustees breached their fiduciary duties to the ESOP by paying excessive salaries to themselves, thereby causing a diminution in the value of the ESOP stock.

The court stated that there does not exist a precise test for determining what a reasonable level of compensation is. While the court noted that the IRS considers levels of compensation exceeding 90% of the median compensation paid to similarly situated executives at comparable companies to be worth a further look, it held that that a comparison of compensation paid at comparable companies is not dispositive. The court stated that many factors, including difficulties involved in the job, responsibilities, earnings, profits, prosperity, qualifications, general economic conditions, and the size and complexities of the business are some additional factors, among others, that must be considered.

The court then held that the determination of salaries was a business decision of the employer that does not involve the administration of an ERISA plan or the involvement of an ERISA plan's assets. Therefore, this determination did not implicate fiduciary concerns. Accordingly, the defendants were not acting in their capacity as fiduciaries of the ESOP when they determined compensation levels for themselves. However, it appears that one of the facts that helped the court reach this decision is that the court found the compensation to be reasonable. The court gave much weight to the fact that Watson Wyatt had been retained to provide a compensation study and that it concluded that compensation levels were not unreasonable. The study noted that all employees at the company were well-paid. In fact, the court gave weight to Watson Wyatt's conclusion that management was not receiving unreasonable compensation and that the stock had generated high returns for the ESOP participants.

The holding of the court that the setting of executive compensation does not implicate fiduciary duties and concerns under ERISA is troubling. The court avoided the issue that the *Delta Star* court addressed. We believe that if an executive who is an ESOP trustee sets executive compensation at unreasonably high levels that unfairly dilute the value of the ESOP stock, he or she will be hard-pressed to defend an action for breach of fiduciary duty by using an *Eckelkamp*-type defense, i.e., that the setting of executive compensation was not a fiduciary concern. We also believe that the *Eckelkamp* decision rested on the fact that the levels of executive compensation were ultimately found to be reasonable and were supported by the report of a third-party expert. We further believe that absent a finding that the executive compensation was reasonable, it is likely the court would have found that there was a breach of fiduciary duty, just as the *Delta Star* court did.

## Determination of Reasonableness of Compensation

It is not the ESOP trustee's duty to set compensation levels at the sponsor company. The board of directors, or a compensation committee of the board of directors, often sets compensation levels for officers of the company. It is the ESOP trustee's duty in its monitoring of the company and management to determine whether the value of the ESOP shares is being negatively affected by excessive compensation levels. If the ESOP trustee determines that executive compensation is unreasonable and unfairly dilutive, then, as the *Delta Star* opinion provides, it is also the ESOP trustee's job to take action to prevent this result.

The first question, then, that needs to be answered is whether the compensation is unreasonable and unfairly dilutive to the shares owned by the ESOP. Practically speaking, the ESOP trustee will rely on its financial advisor or a third-party compensation specialist to make this determination. There is no hard-and-fast rule about what is reasonable and what is not. This determination is purely a facts and circumstances analysis. For example, it may be reasonable to award executives options that dilute the ESOP shares by 10% to 15% if the company has achieved certain performance targets due to the incentive provided by the option program, and the returns to the ESOP shares are acceptable to the ESOP trustee. In these cases, the ESOP is not harmed because presumably it has a smaller piece of a bigger, and more valuable, pie. If the company has achieved little or no growth in equity value, an award of options that have a 15% dilutive impact may be unreasonable.

If the ESOP trustee or its financial advisor are unsure about whether the compensation levels are reasonable, the trustee can suggest that management conduct a compensation study. This study should be conducted by an independent consultant. The purpose of the study is to determine whether the compensation paid to executives is within a reasonable range of market levels. All compensation, including synthetic equity, change of control payments, retention bonuses, and other perquisites, not just salary and bonus, should be considered. The study should compare the compensation paid to executives at the subject company with the compensation paid to executives at comparable companies. However, as the *Eckelkamp* decision suggests, other factors must be taken into account, such as performance, the size of the company relative to its peers, the complexity of the job, responsibilities, and so on.

If executive compensation is determined by a compensation committee of the board of directors that is comprised of independent directors (i.e., directors who are not employees and who otherwise have no affiliation with, or receive no compensation other than as a director from, the company), then the ESOP trustee and its financial advisor will often defer to the decisions of that committee. Under corporate law, directors have a fiduciary duty that is owed to the shareholders of the company. If a committee comprised of independent directors sets executive compensation, then the ESOP trustee can take some comfort that compensation is fair and reasonable and that the board's fiduciary duty to the shareholders is being complied with. Of course, the trustee will still need to monitor the levels of executive compensation to ensure they are reasonable.

## The Trustee's Actions

The actions an ESOP trustee may take can be most easily defined under three distinct scenarios: (1) a transaction in which the ESOP is purchasing stock, (2) a transaction in which the ESOP is selling stock, and (3) ongoing monitoring to determine whether the value of the ESOP stock is negatively affected by executive compensation levels.

First, it should be noted that an ESOP trustee has the most leverage to negotiate executive compensation issues during a transaction in which the ESOP is purchasing stock, particularly in the initial ESOP transaction. When an ESOP purchases stock, the ESOP trustee should require that its financial advisor issue an opinion that (1) it is paying not more than adequate consideration for the stock, and (2) the terms of the transaction are fair to the ESOP from a financial point of view. The second prong of the opinion includes an analysis of executive compensation. If management is receiving compensation that is deemed to be excessive, then even though the ESOP trustee is purchasing stock at a price that is not more than adequate consideration, the trustee still may have a problem completing the transaction and may be unable to obtain the necessary fairness opinion from its financial advisor.

The ESOP trustee can require that executive compensation be set at levels that are fair to the ESOP participants as a condition to purchasing the stock. The trustee can accomplish this by requiring that the executives enter into employment agreements that outline the compensation packages to be paid to them following the closing. The ESOP trustee also can require that the synthetic equity incentive programs for executives be in place before the closing. This way, the ESOP trustee's financial advisor can fully account for executive compensation in his or her analysis of the fairness of the transaction. The ESOP trustee also can negotiate that any changes or amendments to these executive compensation arrangements that would negatively affect the value of the ESOP stock require its consent. Therefore, for example, if the board of directors decided to increase the number of options and SARs for management six months after the ESOP's purchase of stock, the board would have to obtain the ESOP trustee's consent to do this. The existence of this contractual protection for the ESOP does not mean that management is hindered from reaping some of the increased value it has created. Since it is often in the best interests of the ESOP trustee to align its interests with those of management, it will often be the case that the ESOP trustee will consent to some reasonable increase in the amount of synthetic equity that management can receive if the facts and circumstances warrant an increase.

The ESOP trustee also may require that meaningful increases in compensation levels or other forms of executive compensation can be awarded only if certain performance targets are met. In this scenario, the interests of the executives and the ESOP trustee are closely aligned, e.g., growth in earnings creates benefits for the ESOP because of an enhanced stock value and for the executives because their compensation is increased accordingly. Again, the ESOP trustee should be comfortable to share some of the increase in value with management because management has caused the value of the ESOP stock to increase. The ESOP trustee may also suggest that any synthetic equity to be issued to management be of the type that has value only should the value of the company increase. For example, if the board of directors proposes that the executive team be awarded phantom stock, the trustee may suggest that the executives be awarded a reasonable level of SARs rather than phantom stock because for the SARs to have meaningful value, management must cause the value of the company to increase, thereby benefiting everyone. Phantom stock has more value than SARs immediately following its issuance, regardless of whether the value of the company increases, because its economic value is equal to a share of stock.

Executive compensation will also be an issue in the context of a sale of the company. It is not uncommon for management to negotiate transaction success bonuses, change of control payments, or some form of synthetic equity of the purchaser. In the case of a sale of company stock, the ESOP trustee will seek to have its financial advisor issue to it an opinion that (1) the price received for the stock is not less than adequate consideration, and (2) the terms of the transaction are fair to the ESOP from a financial point of view. As in the case of a purchase of stock by the ESOP, executive compensation affects the second element of this opinion. Therefore, the trustee first needs to determine whether these payments made to management in connection with the transaction are really a *disguised purchase price* that should otherwise be shared with the ESOP. If the trustee determines that these payments are really elements of the purchase price that should otherwise be shared with the ESOP, it must negotiate to ensure the ESOP is receiving its fair share of the total sale proceeds. Of course, the trustee's primary negotiating leverage is that it must receive a fairness opinion from its financial advisor.

In addition to monitoring executive compensation when the ESOP is purchasing or selling stock, the ESOP trustee has an obligation to monitor executive compensation in connection with the ongoing fiduciary duty to monitor the management of the ESOP company. In general, the ESOP trustee's leverage on executive compensation outside of the context of a purchase or sale of stock is limited. Nonetheless, the ESOP trustee has an obligation under ERISA to continue to monitor executive compensation and take action on behalf of ESOP participants if it is deemed that the value of the ESOP stock is unduly diluted as a result of excessive compensation. Furthermore, there are actions the ESOP trustee can and should take under such circumstances. The ESOP trustee can contact management directly and discuss its concerns about compensation. The trustee may also contact the board of directors to discuss its concerns. It may request that a compensation committee comprised of independent directors determine compensation. In any case, the ESOP trustee should ensure that it has properly documented the steps it has taken, since the trustee's process is paramount.

Of course, the trustee can also choose to exercise any of the legal rights afforded to corporate shareholders. These rights include the appointment and removal of board members. If the ESOP holds at least a majority of the voting stock, the ESOP trustee can vote to remove directors who refuse to make fair adjustments to compensation that has been deemed to be unreasonable and unfairly dilutive to the ESOP stock and appoint new directors. If the ESOP holds a minority position, the ESOP trustee can still vote to remove these board members, but there is no guarantee that enough of the other shares will be voted in favor of their removal. If the trustee does not act to remove board members in some cases, then it may be faced with a claim of breach of its fiduciary duty, similar to that against the defendant trustee in *Delta Star*. Further, in egregious cases the ESOP trustee also must consider bringing a derivative action, as the *Delta Star* court suggested.

## Conclusion

Executive compensation is a complicated issue that ESOP trustees must deal with to protect the value of the ESOP stock. If management has done its job in growing the value of the stock, the ESOP trustee may share an appropriate level of the economic upside with management. However, when the excessive compensation awarded to management adversely affects the ESOP stock, the trustee has a fiduciary duty under ERISA to take appropriate action to protect the value of the stock.

## Notes

1.   29 U.S.C. § 1104(a)(1)(A)(i).

2.   *Morse v. Stanley*, 732 F.2d 1139, 1145 (2d. Cir. 1984).

3.   76 F. Supp. 2d 617 (W.D. Pa. 1999).

4.   201 F. Supp. 2d 1012 (E.D. Mo.), aff'd, 315 F.3d 863 (8th Cir. 2002).

# CHAPTER 6

# Thoughts on Compensating ESOP Company Executives

**Anthony Mathews**

To begin with, let me state for the record that this chapter is not prompted by any sense that there are compensation inequities in the employee stock ownership plan (ESOP) community. On the contrary, my experience (and the results reported in this book) indicate that in the main, ESOP executives are very modestly compensated relative to their equivalents in non-ESOP companies. Over the years, I have done dozens of compensation studies for ESOP companies, and I have only run across one situation in which the compensation proposed for the CEO was above the 90th percentile for executives in similar situations. Most often, the salary and incentive packages proposed for ESOP company CEOs, as I've seen them, are near or below the mean for similar positions, even though, in my estimation, the executives involved are among the most talented and dedicated people in the market place.

I have stated elsewhere and continue to believe that one of the most significant vulnerabilities of employee ownership as a capital ownership structure is its dependence on selfless, enlightened, and dedicated leadership. Fortunately, it is also our great blessing that the ESOP community has been able to find many such individuals. Or, more likely, they find us. In either case, this chapter doesn't come from any concern for the way in which ESOP companies are compensating their highest-level employees. In the main, I think they are worth much more than they get. Rather, what I am trying for here is a guide to setting compensation strategies for your employee-owned company that can give you comfort that what you are doing is appropriate, both for the executive involved and for the company and its employee owners.

It is a difficult task for the leaders of any company to strike an appropriate balance between offering enough compensation for a particular job to attract the greatest people to fill it; creating incentive programs to both encourage and reward high levels of performance; and, at the same time, maximizing the value created for the owners. I know there are a number of underlying assumptions here that may or may not be real. For example, it may well be that great people are not motivated by money or power, but by love of accomplishing something worthwhile. I'd like to think that things like that are true, but history and experience say otherwise, so for now I think we have to go with what we know.

Attraction, retention, and performance are, to a great extent, at least, going to be determined by the compensation packages we offer, and the highest-level executives in our companies are going to have a significant influence on how successful we can become.

Having said that, when we look at the process of formulating a compensation program or strategy, there are clear conflicts among the masters being served, no matter how the ownership of the company is vested. The potential conflict of interest between corporate officers' salary and incentive desires on the one hand, and the earnings desires of shareholders on the other, is an old problem that is revisited constantly in all areas of the financial marketplace. In most traditional closely held corporations, though, the key management employees comprise the same group as the shareholders (or at least a closely related group) and so the conflicts are relatively easily resolved. In public companies, (although recent experience seems to impeach its effectiveness) the oversight of the accounting community, SEC, and the public market gives at least some comfort that the shareholder interests are being protected.

In an employee ownership company, neither external safeguard exists. The guardians of the corporate value are most often the management executives of the company (and their agents), and finding the right balance between their personal financial interest and the best interests of the shareholders can be particularly tricky. Obviously, where the management employees of the company are also the only fiduciaries to its ERISA-protected retirement plan, which happens also to be a substantial (often even majority or only) shareholder, the potential conflicts of interest are many and can seem insurmountable. Yet surmount them we must if, as employee ownership companies in this situation, we are to compete successfully for the most talented executives in a world that is, in the main, largely unimpressed by the fact that we are employee-owned.

I'll reiterate for the last time here, that there may, in fact, be many very talented executives who would not be suitable to lead an employee ownership company no matter what the compensation package looks like. I have, over the years, met many such individuals who were arguably great managers and skilled business strategists but who were totally unsuited to the role of leader in an employee ownership company. So it may be that in some cases, the interests of a particular executive will simply be incompatible with the employee ownership model, and we will have to look elsewhere.

Nevertheless, the problem of creating appropriate compensation packages when we do find suitable executives continues to persist. This basic problem is considerably exacerbated by the nature and terms of many ESOP transactions that commit high levels of equity, future earnings, cash flow, and other financial resources to a project that is unprofitable and that often brings the most key management personnel very little, if any, direct benefit. In fact, many ESOP transactions actually damage the non-selling management employees' net worth, resources, and terms of employment. Clearly, we cannot let the ESOP become a significant disincentive for management. Designing around these problems is a real challenge for every ESOP company.

I think the answer has to be careful selection and planning, effective use of outsiders (consultants and/or outside directors) to make and/or support key decisions, and thorough documentation of your ongoing due diligence. There is nothing inherent in an ESOP company that requires management to accept less for the same effort than it would expect from an equivalent non-ESOP company, but it seems to work out that way. The key is figuring out and documenting exactly what that means.

## Where to Begin

As in any company, I think an ESOP company should begin the exploration of compensation issues with an examination of its objectives and a comprehensive understanding of the compensation philosophy those objectives imply. This might take the form of a comprehensive compensation statement. This statement could incorporate the company's goals and objectives and basically lay out a philosophy of compensation that is designed to approach those goals. Formulating a compensation philosophy statement may seem like an academic exercise, but if comprehensively done, it can save considerable time and effort and minimize potential misunderstandings among all concerned. More important, it can serve as the basis for developing an overall compensation strategy and specific compensation programs for specific executives.

Also, as in any organization, each ESOP company will have its own focal points, areas in which the company wants to encourage or discourage activity. These individual interests will be reflected in both the process and the outcome, and the practical objective will be to formalize the company's position on specific compensation arrangements in order to foster those goals.

In general, every company's compensation strategy will reflect its philosophy (and ESOP companies are not usually exceptions) and can be described in terms of the following ratios (whether consciously included in the process or not.) And, in turn, the ratios can play a significant role in determining the specifics of the resulting compensation strategy.

- *Secure vs. At-Risk:* The ratio of secure compensation to at-risk compensation is the first spectrum to be considered. With neither positive nor negative judgment implied, this ratio reflects a company's attitude toward its growth potential, its sense of employees' contributions to growth, and its sense of obligation to and relationship with its employees. Secure compensation is basically that compensation that is dependent only on the employee's meeting the minimum requirements for continued employment. At-risk compensation is compensation that relies on either indi-

vidual or group achievements (or both.) Commission is probably the oldest form of at-risk compensation, and in many ways,
it is a good key to determining at-risk incentives even where a
specific commission structure would not be appropriate. These
generally take the form of base and incentive compensation, in
common terms. For this purpose, generally, higher-level executives in entrepreneurial companies will tend to have higher per-
centages of at-risk pay.

- *Short-Term vs. Long-Term:* The ratio of immediate or short-term
  compensation to deferred or long-term compensation is the second feature of the compensation equation. While to some extent
  this overlaps at-risk and/or secure compensation, there will be a
  mix of short and long-term incentive values that should also be
  considered. Retirement benefits are obviously a long- term incentive, but we can find long-term elements in virtually every aspect
  of compensation. Direct base salary, for example, is definitely a
  short-term incentive; however, salary increase policies (which are
  certainly part of a complete compensation strategy) are long-term
  components. In any case, the mix of short and long-term elements
  also reflects the company's attitude and intentions, and it should
  be a logical outgrowth of the compensation statement.

- *Cash vs. In-kind Compensation:* In any compensation philosophy,
  there will be a mix of cash compensation (e.g. salary, cash bonuses, etc.) and other non-cash types of compensation (e.g. fringe
  benefits, stock options, etc.)

- *Formula vs. Discretionary Rewards:* For most small to medium-sized
  business owners, one of the most difficult transitions is from purely
  discretionary incentives (i.e. annual bonuses figured by management on a subjective basis) to more formula-based approaches
  through which individual employees can have a more direct impact on their rewards.

Without regard to the ownership structure, older, more established
companies frequently arrive at a focus on secure cash compensation
and long-term incentive types of pay (e.g., established salary scales,
pension-type retirement plans, tenure-related term bonuses, or stock

option programs). Newer or more entrepreneurial companies often concentrate on short-term incentives and at-risk, in-kind types of compensation (e.g., profit sharing, salary reduction stock plans, commission-based pay scales, or stock option programs). Formula vs. discretionary remains a factor of personality at all ages. At any point, however, rethinking the compensation structure along these lines can be very instructive. We must not forget the particular effects of our ownership structure as well. In today's environment (especially in ESOP companies), deferred compensation has taken on new complexities and created new concerns. It may be, for example, that in an ESOP owned S corporation, traditional long-term and deferred compensation strategies will create all sorts of qualification concerns that must be honored.

Consideration of these factors can be particularly instructive where an ESOP transaction has caused a significant shift in the focus of a company, which, almost certainly, has many agreements, programs, contracts, and even expectations already in place with employees that may or may not fit in with the new ESOP direction.

## The Comfort of Benchmarks

A first stop many take on the way to an effective compensation package is to determine the range of levels and types of compensation that are typical for your particular situation. Research has shown that compensation and incentive packages vary dramatically based on the demographics of each company. Compensation and incentive for a particular job title will vary considerably based on the industry, geographic location, revenue, and profitability. There are several private and public databases for this purpose, but in most cases you will need to consult a compensation specialist.

In any case, the important reference points are the overall level of compensation; the mix of base vs. incentive pay, current vs. deferred pay, and secure vs. at-risk pay; and the nature of compensation paid. It is most important to adjust the data for industry (getting comparisons in the same or similar SIC code is usually sufficient), geographic references (identical job classifications can vary as much as 25% or more simply based on location), the size of your company, and the specific job description. Other, more subjective, adjustments can also come into play, such as extraordinary earnings. With the help of this text and some recent research, you can also now include some reference points within the employee ownership community.

It is important to keep in mind that the comparison groups do not create any obligation to conform one way or the other. A particular ESOP company's executive compensation can take any form or level the parties agree is appropriate. The real value of benchmarking with a comparison group is to establish a range of reasonable levels and types of compensation for different job classifications and to demonstrate due diligence on the part of whoever is making the decisions.

## Special ESOP Considerations

With ESOPs, we get a sizable basket of specifically ESOP issues to address. This is particularly true where the ESOP is a majority shareholder; more so where the ESOP has provided Internal Revenue Code Section 1042 rollover benefits to the seller; and even more so with the growing trend to create 100% ESOP-owned S corporations. In all these cases, key executive employees may not only have their continuing compensation to concern them but may have suffered serious reverses along the way as well.

### ESOPs Sometimes Seem to Imply Limits on Competitive Compensation Packages

No one disagrees that an ESOP company must compete for talented personnel in a sometimes limited market. As we look at the methods most companies use to attract and retain employees, many are either intuitively inappropriate, financially impractical, or arguably illegal when a company is owned substantially by an ESOP. Yet, if ESOP companies are to survive and succeed in the world which is largely unimpressed with our employee ownership, ways to do so must be found. Typically, this means that the ESOP trustees, just like other shareholders, may have to create special programs outside of the qualified plan arena. Indeed, the trustees may have to share ownership with these key executives to keep their level of incentive as high as desirable and properly compensate them for their contributions to the process.

## Section 1042 Is a Great Blessing for Sellers but Sometimes Is Bad News for Those Left Behind

It is very common for a substantial or majority shareholder to establish a leveraged ESOP for purposes of setting up a rollover and deferral of gain on the sale of his or her stock. Several side effects of that transaction are relevant here. Key executive personnel at an ESOP company often find themselves in a significantly worse position after the transaction. First, the debt burden taken on by the company usually reduces the ability of the company to continue to fund special bonuses. This would be bad enough if it were fully offset by ESOP participation, but most often these key employees' participation in the ESOP is cut back because of the legal limits on compensation that may be used for plan purposes. Where these key employees are either related to the seller or shareholders in their own right, the matter just gets worse. Often, these key people will not only be limited in the ESOP, they may well be eliminated altogether. Finally, adding yet another injury, on top of the fact that a key employee's ownership interest in the company may have the effect of prohibiting ESOP participation, that key employee will probably also has seen a significant decrease in his or her equity value as a result of the decrease in value of the company brought about by the leverage.

There is no perfect solution for these problems. It does take a dedication on the part of remaining management to the ESOP concept to make it work. Some steps can, and should, be taken, though, to insure equitable treatment for these people. Without them, even if an ESOP deal is somehow made to occur, the company will very likely not survive or at least will have serious problems to overcome.

## ESOP Lenders May Prefer Some Outside Ownership

Frequently, the very existence of the ESOP itself requires the creation of ownership interest among a class of management employees outside of the ERISA-protected trust fund. Where the only shareholder in a company is legally prohibited from guaranteeing the debt of the corporation (as is the case in a 100% ESOP company), it is sometimes difficult to get lender interest in banking the company. And, for obvious reasons, it is often difficult to come up with a convincing rationale for a non-shareholder manager to do so, even assuming the bank were willing to accept that. To be sure, many such managers have stepped up to the plate over the years, but even where that has been the case, the inequity is a clear one, and ESOP companies cannot afford to rely on the altruism of a very small pool of such managers.

## In Transition, We Always Confront Existing Agreements and Important Expectations

On top of any legal or financial issues that arise, most companies have formal (or even informal) agreements with management employees that may or may not be compatible with the existence of the ESOP. Promises of stock ownership interest to several key employees are fairly common, but if they are not firmly in place by the time the ESOP is installed, the entire process can well be reset to zero. One very important part of any ESOP installation is determining the extent of these issues and structuring programs to address them.

## In S Corporations, Current Law Provides Both Challenges and Opportunities

As everyone knows by now, 1998 was a banner year for the employee ownership movement. As of that year, ESOPs became qualified shareholders in S corporations. This created many planning opportunities for ESOP companies, and S corporations are among the most active areas in ESOP growth. The benefits of this structure can be most thoroughly used where an ESOP is the 100% shareholder. This, in turn, created a trend to revisiting restricted stock and stock-equivalent equity compensation programs to provide vehicles to facilitate or create 100% ESOP ownership where key employees and executives might otherwise want or deserve ownership interests outside of the ESOP.

At the same time, the Economic Growth and Tax Relief Reconciliation Act of 2001 added a new wrinkle to this equation. Under the provisions of Internal Revenue Code Section 409(p) (and subsequent regulations), a concentration of "deemed-owned shares" among certain owners of the company can cause the ESOP S corporation. to lose its significant tax advantage (and a lot of other really bad things to happen as well). For this purpose, "deemed-owned shares" includes ESOP stock as well as other "synthetic equity," and that is the rub, because for this purpose, "synthetic equity" includes everything from real stock options to SARs and phantom stock and even to any contingent right to receive stock or deferred compensation agreement. Add to that the changes introduced to deferred compensation plans in general with the American Jobs Creation Act of 2004, and a real need for caution is clear in this area.

So, if you are an S corporation or are considering becoming one, and you either already have some of these programs in place or are considering using one of these vehicles in some way (e.g., in converting a key employee's stock ownership into nonqualified stock-equivalent benefit such as a phantom stock plan, or creating incidental stock holdings whose shares are considered unissued for federal tax purposes), you will have to be very careful not to grant equity interests that will cause the penalties to kick in.

The intricacies of all of this testing are beyond treatment in this chapter (see chapter 2 for more information), but please note that if you are an S corporation with an ESOP, you will have to make at least one additional stop before you finalize any sort of executive incentive plan. That stop will be with your ESOP administrator or attorney to be sure that what you are intending to implement will not be in violation of these rules.

### In the End, It Is a Constant Process of Identifying and Avoiding Fiduciary Conflicts of Interest

In resolving all these problems, ESOP company management face clear and difficult conflict issues. Even if they are allowed to participate in the ESOP, management employees will almost invariably be both employees with their own self interest (which may or may not be identical to the interest of the shareholders) and fiduciaries who are specifically charged with a significant responsibility for the well being of shareholders who are not usually in a position to look after themselves.

In general, ESOP company management employees should never be in the position of unilaterally making up their own compensation package. Outside directors are a very useful addition to the board of any ESOP company, if for no other reason than to establish an arguably objective compensation committee. ESOP company management and directors should consistently abstain from decisions where the conflict of interest exists because even where an objective third party might have reached the same decision, the act of a conflicted party is automatically suspect and must be proven to be reasonable and consistent with the fiduciary duty to shareholders and to plan participants under ERISA. That is obviously much more difficult than defending the decision of a disinterested (or at least non-conflicted) party.

Outside directors and constant use of competent, recognized professional advisors is a virtual must for an ESOP company to avoid these pitfalls.

## Conclusion

Designing compensation strategies in ESOP companies is not really any different from doing so in any other company, but the fact of our ownership structure creates additional responsibilities for care in decision making. Incentive program design for an ESOP company is more complicated than in non-ESOP equivalent circumstances to be sure, but the issues are exactly the same. The complication comes, just as in many other areas of corporate life, from the special relationship that develops among employees, management, and shareholders in ESOP companies. Like so many of the special problems ESOPs face, the difficulty involved in designing and implementing both prudent and effective compensation programs comes directly from the very features that give them extraordinary strength. An appropriate program is achievable safely, however, if ESOP trustees and other fiduciaries follow a few fairly straightforward guidelines:

- Deal with compensation issues objectively and as early as possible in the process.

- Recognize the contributions of key management (specifically where their compensation, benefits and equity have been compromised by the establishment of the plan), and design a program accordingly.

- Make liberal use of outside directors and consultants to demonstrate due diligence.
- Use the benchmark approach to validate program designs.
- Document the decision making process and, as closely as possible, foster what amounts to a negotiation of terms.

As with any company, ESOP companies rely on the good faith and incentive of employees at all levels. So, even in the arena of executive compensation, we can and should strive for a win-win outcome for all concerned.

# About the Authors

**Virginia Bartlett** has over 25 years of experience in working with all types of employee benefit programs. Her background includes serving as an employee plans specialist with the Employee Plans/Exempt Organizations Division of the Internal Revenue Service as well as an investigator with the Office of Enforcement at the U.S. Department of Labor's Pension and Welfare Benefits Administration. She has extensive experience in designing and implementing employee benefit programs, consulting on mergers and acquisitions issues that relate to employee benefit plan issues, and conducting IRS and ERISA compliance reviews. Before establishing Bartlett O'Neill Consulting, Inc., Virginia was a senior vice president in Clark Consulting's Human Capital practice, where she was a member of the Employee Benefits Consulting group and in charge of the national Retirement Plans group. Before that, Virginia was a partner with Arthur Andersen, where she was a member of the firm's Retirement, Actuarial, and Benefits service line in its Human Capital practice, where she led the ERISA Special Services practice. She was recruited by David M. Walker to join Andersen's Human Capital Practice in 1987. When Mr. Walker left Andersen to assume his duties as Comptroller General for the United States, Ms. Bartlett was recognized as the national practice leader for the ERISA Special Services practice.

**Marilyn H. Marchetti** is a senior vice president at GreatBanc Trust Company, where she heads the ESOP Services Group. Ms. Marchetti joined GreatBanc Trust Company in 1999. She began her career more than 20 years ago as an attorney, specializing in employee benefits law. She has worked exclusively with ESOPs and has represented clients, including Fortune 500 companies, in virtually every aspect of ESOP transactions. Ms. Marchetti was instrumental in developing and structuring international ESOPs for multinational U.S. corporations and has been a featured speaker at ESOP conferences in the United States, Europe, China, and Africa. A former member of the board of directors of the ESOP Association, she currently participates on its board of governors. She also chairs the Fiduciary Subcommittee of the Legislative and Regulatory Committee of the ESOP Association. Ms. Marchetti founded the Illinois chapter of the ESOP Association and served as its chapter secretary and treasurer.

**Anthony Mathews** is an officer with Principal Financial Group. He is a senior consultant and second vice president in the Employer Securities Consulting area of Retirement and Investor Services. Tony has spent 25 years as an ESOP consultant and principal in several of the most respected firms in ESOP consulting and recordkeeping, and he is a frequent speaker and often-published authority on a wide variety of topics related to the design, implementation, administration, and operation of ESOPs. He is a member of the NCEO's board of directors, a founding member of the Administrative Advisory Committee of the ESOP Association, a former director of the ESOP Association, a member of the steering committee of the California/Western States chapter of the ESOP Association, an associate member of the American Society of Pension Actuaries, and is heavily involved in many other pension- and employee ownership-related organizations.

**Helen H. Morrison** is a principal with Deloitte Tax LLP. She is the national leader of the firm's ESOP Advisory Services Practice and the Midwest regional practice leader for Employee Benefits Tax. Ms. Morrison concentrates her practice in executive compensation, qualified retirement plans, ESOPs, and business succession planning. Ms. Morrison is a frequent speaker and author on equity-based compensation programs, ESOPs, and business succession planning. She is the coauthor of several books and articles on topics related to ESOPs, executive compensation, and global equity plans. Ms. Morrison is an adjunct professor of law in the Employee Benefits Master of Tax program at John Marshall Law School. Before joining Deloitte, Ms. Morrison was a partner at the international law firm of McDermott, Will & Emery, resident in the firm's Chicago office.

**Alan A. Nadel** serves as the managing director of Alan Nadel & Company LLC, a compensation consulting firm based in New York. He has more than 33 years of experience serving a diverse range of clients, advising on matters relating to executive and board of directors compensation, employee benefits, retirement benefit programs, and income and estate planning. He advises clients on the various aspects of these programs, including the strategic, financial, accounting, and tax considerations. Before establishing his company, Alan was a partner in two major accounting firms and was a principal with an actuarial and benefits consulting firm. This included establishing and building the Human Capital practice at Arthur Andersen LLP, where he served as the managing partner for Human Capital. Previously he was with the Internal Revenue Service. Alan is a coauthor of the *Employee Benefits Handbook*. He is a frequent speaker before professional and industry groups

**Christine Robovsky** is a manager in Deloitte Consulting's Human Capital practice. She has over five years of experience working with companies on a wide range of executive and broad-based compensation issues, including the assessment of competitive pay levels, incentive compensation plan design, and board of director compensation.

**Corey Rosen** is the executive director and cofounder of the National Center for Employee Ownership (NCEO), a private, nonprofit membership, information, and research organization in Oakland, CA. The NCEO is widely considered to be the authoritative source on broad-based employee ownership plans. He cofounded the NCEO in 1981 after working for five years as a professional staff member in the U.S. Senate, where he helped draft legislation on employee ownership plans.

Before that, he taught political science at Ripon College. He is the author or coauthor of many books and over 100 articles on employee ownership, and co-author (with John Case) of *Equity: Why Employee Ownership Is Good for Business* (Harvard Business School Press, 2005). He was the subject of an extensive interview in *Inc.* magazine in August 2000, has appeared frequently on CNN, PBS, NPR, and other network programs, and is regularly quoted in *The Wall Street Journal, The New York Times,* and other leading publications.

**James E. Staruck** is a vice president in the ESOP Services Group at GreatBanc Trust Company, where he specializes in ESOP transactions. He joined GreatBanc Trust Company in 2004. Before joining GreatBanc Trust, he practiced law at a large Chicago law firm, where he focused on mergers and acquisitions, including acquisitions and sales of privately held companies by ESOPs, debt and equity financings, and general corporate law.

**Julie A. Williams** is a vice president at GreatBanc Trust Company, where she specializes in ESOP transactional analysis. Ms. Williams joined GreatBanc Trust in 2004. Before joining GreatBanc Trust, Ms. Williams was a financial advisor with Duff & Phelps, LLC, where she worked on business valuations, fairness opinions, and a variety of corporate finance and strategic advisory engagements involving ESOPs. Ms. Williams also provided corporate advisory services as a consultant with Arthur Andersen LLC and was an investment analyst in the trust department of Amoco Corporation

# About the NCEO

The National Center for Employee Ownership (NCEO) is widely considered to be the leading authority in employee ownership in the U.S. and the world. Established in 1981 as a nonprofit information and membership organization, it now has over 2,500 members. It is funded entirely through the work it does. The NCEO's mission is to provide the most objective, reliable information possible about employee ownership at the most affordable price possible. The NCEO publishes a variety of materials explaining how employee ownership plans work, describing how companies get employee owners more involved in making decisions about their work, and reviewing the research on employee ownership. In addition, the NCEO holds dozens of seminars, Webinars, and conferences on employee ownership annually, maintains extensive contacts with the media, writes and edits books for other publishers, and has a large Web site at *www.nceo.org.*

*NCEO Membership* NCEO members receive (1) the bimonthly newsletter *Employee Ownership Report,* which covers both ESOPs and equity compensation; (2) access to the members-only area of the NCEO Web site *(www.nceo.org),* which features a variety of online resources; (3) discounts on NCEO publications and events; and (4) the right to telephone the NCEO for answers to general or specific questions regarding employee ownership. It costs $80 to join the NCEO for one year.

# Selected NCEO Publications

The NCEO offers a variety of publications on all aspects of employee ownership and participation, from employee stock ownership plans (ESOPs) to stock options to employee participation. Below are descriptions of some of our main publications.

We publish new books and revise old ones on a yearly basis. To obtain the most current information on what we have available, visit our Web site at *www.nceo.org* or call us at 510-208-1300.

## Employee Stock Ownership Plans (ESOPs)

- This book, *Executive Compensation in ESOP Companies,* includes essays on the subject as well as a summary of a survey that measured how ESOP company executives are being compensated.

  $25 for NCEO members, $35 for nonmembers

- *The ESOP Reader* is an overview of the issues involved in establishing and operating an ESOP. It covers the basics of ESOP rules, feasibility, valuation, and other matters, and then discusses managing an ESOP company, including brief case studies. The book is intended for those with a general interest in ESOPs.

  $25 for NCEO members, $35 for nonmembers

- *Selling to an ESOP* is a guide for owners, managers, and advisors of closely held businesses. It explains how ESOPs work and then offers a comprehensive look at legal structures, valuation, financing (including self-financing), and other matters, especially the tax-deferred section 1042 "rollover."

  $25 for NCEO members, $35 for nonmembers

- *Leveraged ESOPs and Employee Buyouts* discusses how ESOPs borrow money to buy out entire companies, purchase shares from a retiring owner, or finance new capital. Beginning with a primer on leveraged ESOPs and their uses, it then discusses contribution limits, valuation, accounting, feasibility, financing, and more.

  $25 for NCEO members, $35 for nonmembers

- The *Model ESOP* provides a sample ESOP plan, with alternative provisions given to tailor the plan to individual needs. It also includes a section-by-section explanation of the plan and other supporting materials.

  $50 for NCEO members, $75 for nonmembers

- *ESOP Valuation* brings together and updates where needed the best articles on ESOP valuation that we have published in our *Journal of Employee Ownership Law and Finance,* described below.

  $25 for NCEO members, $35 for nonmembers

- *How ESOP Companies Handle the Repurchase Obligation* has essays and recent research on the subject.

  $25 for NCEO members, $35 for nonmembers

- *The ESOP Committee Guide* describes the different types of ESOP committees, the range of goals they can address, alternative structures, member selection criteria, training, committee life cycle concerns, and other issues.

  $25 for NCEO members, $35 for nonmembers

- *Wealth and Income Consequences of Employee Ownership* is a detailed report on a comparative study of ESOP companies in Washington State that found ESOP companies pay more and provided better benefits than other companies.

  $10 for NCEO members, $15 for nonmembers

- *ESOPs and Corporate Governance* covers everything from shareholder rights to the impact of Sarbanes-Oxley to choosing a fiduciary.

  $25 for NCEO members, $35 for nonmembers

- *The ESOP Communications Sourcebook* provides ideas for and examples of communicating an ESOP to employees and customers. It includes a CD with communications materials, including many documents that readers can customize for their own companies.

  $35 for NCEO members, $50 for nonmembers

## Equity Compensation Plans

- *The Stock Options Book* is a straightforward, comprehensive overview covering the legal, accounting, regulatory, and design issues involved in implementing a stock option or stock purchase plan, including "broad-based" plans covering most or all employees. It is our main book on the subject and possibly the most popular book in the field.

  $25 for NCEO members, $35 for nonmembers

- *Selected Issues in Equity Compensation* is more detailed and specialized than *The Stock Options Book*, with chapters on issues such as repricing, securities issues, and evergreen options. The appendix is an exhaustive glossary of terms used in the field.

  $25 for NCEO members, $35 for nonmembers

- *Beyond Stock Options* is a guide to phantom stock, stock appreciation rights, restricted stock, direct stock purchase plans, and performance awards used as alternatives to stock options.

  $35 for NCEO members, $50 for nonmembers

- *Employee Stock Purchase Plans* covers how ESPPs work, tax and legal issues, administration, accounting, communicating the plan to employees, and research on what companies are doing with their plans.

  $25 for NCEO members, $35 for nonmembers

- *Equity-Based Compensation for Multinational Corporations* describes how companies can use stock options and other equity-based programs across the world to reward a global work force. It includes a country-by-country summary of tax and legal issues.

  $25 for NCEO members, $35 for nonmembers

- *Incentive Compensation and Employee Ownership* takes a broad look at how companies can use incentives, ranging from stock plans to cash bonuses to gainsharing, to motivate and reward employees. It includes both technical discussions and case studies.

  $25 for NCEO members, $35 for nonmembers

## Employee Involvement and Management

- *Ownership Management* draws upon the experience of the NCEO and of leading employee ownership companies to discuss how to build a culture of lasting innovation by combining employee ownership with employee involvement.

  $25 for NCEO members, $35 for nonmembers

## Other

- *Section 401(k) Plans and Employee Ownership* focuses on how company stock is used in 401(k) plans, both in stand-alone 401(k) plans and combination 401(k)–ESOP plans ("KSOPs").

  $25 for NCEO members, $35 for nonmembers

- *Employee Ownership and Corporate Performance* reviews the research that has been done on the link between company stock plans and various aspects of corporate performance.

  $25 for NCEO members, $35 for nonmembers

- *Employee Ownership Concepts in Nonprofits and Government* discusses how nonprofits and governmental units, despite their lack of stock, can implement employee ownership concepts.

  $25 for NCEO members, $35 for nonmembers

- *The Journal of Employee Ownership Law and Finance* is the only professional journal solely devoted to employee ownership. Articles are written by leading experts and cover ESOPs, stock options, and related subjects in depth.

  One-year subscription (four issues):
  $75 for NCEO members, $100 for nonmembers

**To join the NCEO as a member or to order any of the publications listed on the preceding pages, use the order form on the following page, use the secure ordering system on our Web site at *www.nceo.org*, or call us at 510-208-1300. If you join at the same time you order publications, you will receive the members-only publication discounts.**

## Order Form

To order, fill out this form and mail it with your credit card information or check to the NCEO at 1736 Franklin St., 8th Flr., Oakland, CA 94612; fax it with your credit card information to the NCEO at 510-272-9510; telephone us at 510-208-1300 with your credit card in hand; or order securely online at our Web site, *www.nceo.org*. If you are not already a member, you can join now to receive member discounts on the publications you order.

Name

Organization

Address

City, State, Zip (Country)

Telephone                    Fax                              E-mail

**Method of Payment:**   ❏ Check (payable to "NCEO")   ❏ Visa   ❏ M/C   ❏ AMEX

Credit Card Number

Signature                                              Exp. Date

*Checks are accepted only for orders from the U.S. and must be in U.S. currency.*

| Title | Qty. | Price | Total |
|---|---|---|---|
|  |  |  |  |
|  |  |  |  |
|  |  |  |  |
|  |  |  |  |

**Tax:** California residents add 8.75% sales tax (on publications only, not membership or Journal subscriptions)

**Shipping:** In the U.S., first publication $5, each add'l $1; outside the U.S., we charge exact shipping costs to your credit card, plus a $10 handling surcharge; no shipping charges for memberships or Journal subscriptions

**Introductory NCEO Membership:** $80 for one year ($90 outside the U.S.)

| | |
|---|---|
| Subtotal | $ |
| Sales Tax | $ |
| Shipping | $ |
| Membership | $ |
| TOTAL DUE | $ |

# Ordering ESOP Executive Compensation Survey Custom Reports or Data

W hat are the compensation benchmarks for ESOP companies? How much base, deferred, and incentive compensation should top executives at your company expect? What
about stock options, restricted stock, and other forms of equity compensation? The NCEO's ESOP Executive Compensation Database fills
this information gap. Based on a detailed survey of 204 ESOP companies conducted in 2005, the database includes background information about each respondent (company size, age of ESOP, corporate
status, stock growth, industry, etc.), details of compensation mechanics
(vesting, mechanisms to set compensation, perquisites, etc.) and detailed compensation data. (The identities of individual companies are
not revealed.) Chapter 3 of this book provides an overview of the survey
results. However, for data relevant to your own situation, you may
purchase a report that customizes the data to focus on companies comparable to yours, or you may even wish to acquire the entire data set.

## Ordering a Custom Report

A custom report includes two different breakdowns of the data based
on criteria you supply. For example, you might have table 1 look at
manufacturing companies broken down by the number of employees
and table 2 look at manufacturing companies broken down into S

corporations versus C corporations. The report is emailed to you in PDF format. The cost is $150 for NCEO members and $300 for non-members. If you are not an NCEO member but join when you order, you will pay the discounted member price.

## Ordering the Entire Database for Your Own Analyses

ESOP consultants and others may wish to order the entire database (emailed as an Excel spreadsheet file) so that they may run an unlimited number of custom reports. Up to 10 custom reports (produced by the NCEO) are also included. The cost is $1,000 for NCEO members and $2,000 for nonmembers. If you are not an NCEO member but join when you order, you will pay the discounted member price.

## How to Order or Get More Information

To order or get more information, call NCEO Project Director Loren Rodgers at 510-208-1307 or NCEO Executive Director Corey Rosen at 510-208-1314.